RICHARD III
THE KING UNDER THE CAR PARK

The story of the search for England's last Plantagenet king

Mathew Morris and Richard Buckley

University *of* Leicester

Archaeological Services

University of Leicester Archaeological Services (ULAS) is a professional archaeological unit based in the School of Archaeology and Ancient History at the University of Leicester. ULAS undertakes archaeological projects all over the UK, mostly connected with planning applications for new developments, road schemes and quarries. The unit has particular expertise in urban archaeology, and staff have been involved in almost all of the major excavations that have taken place in Leicester over the past 35 years.

ULAS, School of Archaeology and Ancient History, University Road, Leicester LE1 7RH

www.le.ac.uk/ulas

The **School of Archaeology and Ancient History** at the University of Leicester can trace its origins back to 1958 and is one of the foremost archaeology departments in the UK. Undergraduate and postgraduate programmes are offered in Leicester and the school also has a large and thriving Distance Learning community who study at Certificate, undergraduate, Masters and PhD level. Staff have field projects all over the world, exploring the archaeologies of past societies from prehistoric through to early modern times. ULAS and the School together run an annual training excavation for students, currently at the Iron Age hillfort of Burrough Hill in Leicestershire.

School of Archaeology and Ancient History, University Road, Leicester LE1 7RH

www.le.ac.uk/departments/archaeology

The **Richard III Society** was founded in 1924 in the belief that many features of the traditional accounts of the character and career of Richard III are neither supported by sufficient evidence nor reasonably tenable. The Society aims to promote, in every possible way, research into the life and times of Richard III, and to secure a reassessment of the material relating to this period, and of the role of this monarch in English history. The Society has several thousand members worldwide. It operates on many levels and is open to lay people and historians alike. All that is needed is an interest in the life and times of Richard III.

www.richardiii.net

Leicester City Council is the unitary authority serving the people, communities and businesses of Leicester, the biggest city in the East Midlands.

Leicester City Council, New Walk Centre, Welford Place, Leicester LE1 6ZG

www.leicester.gov.uk

Contents

Archaeologist Steve Baker shows members of the public around the Greyfriars site on Saturday 8 September 2012.

Foreword

The discovery of Richard III was a defining moment in the story of Leicester. The search for his mortal remains under a car park made history – and captured headlines across the world. It brought the University of Leicester into close partnership with the City Council, the Cathedral, the Richard III Society and local people – many of whom had queued for hours to view the Greyfriars dig and sent us messages of support and goodwill.

Higher education is about improving lives – empowering people through education and advances in research. Our world-class research in Archaeology, Genetics and Engineering, as well as other subjects, has brought this project to fruition. This story illustrates the power of research to capture our imaginations and advance our knowledge of the historical account of the city and the county. It is that story we recount here.

From the outset, the Search for Richard III was an exciting project that has involved many hours of dedicated research by a team drawn from a number of University departments and has led to the research findings described in this book. That the project was successful in locating the king's remains was in no small part due to the detailed knowledge of the City and its history acquired over many years by the University of Leicester archaeologists.

I would like to pay tribute to my academic colleagues whose outstanding research has delivered this historic discovery and led to this splendid publication. Thanks are due also to our partners, Leicester City Council, Leicester Cathedral, the Richard III Society and especially Philippa Langley, who instigated the project.

Leicester has been congratulated by the Prime Minister, and members of the public have been emailing and writing to us with a deep sense of admiration. The project has engaged schools and many other organisations. My colleagues have attended events around the country, and abroad, to discuss their findings.

It took months of planning and a carefully executed strategy to develop this project. Ultimately, though, success comes not simply from executing a strategy, but from ensuring that everyone pulls together to achieve purposeful impact. The University has demonstrated that research is based upon leadership and teamwork, which the Richard III project has in equal measure.

Professor Sir Robert Burgess
Vice-Chancellor, University of Leicester

The Greyfriars Project: how it all started

In the final battle of the Wars of the Roses at Bosworth Field in Leicestershire on August 22 1485, the Yorkist King Richard III led a fateful cavalry charge and was killed, thereby making Henry Tudor, his adversary, king of England. On the same day Henry – now Henry VII – rode back to Leicester with his army, bringing with him Richard's body which had been unceremoniously slung naked over the back of a horse. Here, it was put on public display so that the inhabitants of the town – who had waved him off to battle only a day or so before – could see for themselves that the king was dead. Shortly afterwards, Richard's body was buried with little ceremony in the church of the Franciscan friars (the Grey Friars) in Leicester. Ten years later, Henry paid for a modest

Above: Medieval re-enactors recreate the Battle of Bosworth during the 2013 Anniversary Weekend at the Bosworth Battlefield Heritage Centre.

tombstone to be placed over Richard's grave. In 1538, the friary was dissolved, the church was demolished and the site eventually passed into the hands of Robert Herrick, a former mayor of Leicester, who had a mansion built there in the early 17th century. Herrick believed that the king's remains still lay in his garden, whilst other rumours circulated at this time that Richard's skeleton had been dug up and thrown into the River Soar by a jeering mob, a belief commonly held by many until the present day. A number of notable historians,

however, thought this highly unlikely and one, David Baldwin, predicted in 1986 that the king's remains might yet be found on the Greyfriars site by archaeologists in the 21st century.

Almost all archaeological excavations undertaken within the city of Leicester to date have been in connection with redevelopment, with the objective of ensuring that important remains are investigated and recorded before they are destroyed or damaged by new buildings. So although there are many sites – like Greyfriars – that archaeologists would dearly like to explore for other reasons, such opportunities rarely present themselves. So it was rather a surprise to Richard Buckley of ULAS when Philippa Langley, a screenwriter and secretary of the Scottish Branch of the Richard III Society, telephoned in January 2011 with the idea of searching for the burial place of Richard III. He said, 'As one who has worked for many years on urban sites in the city, I immediately foresaw all sorts of problems. Most of the precinct of the Franciscan friary was built over, leaving just three areas potentially accessible for investigation: two operational car parks and a former school playground, all of which were probably riddled with live services. Even if we could get access, what were the chances of finding the friary church, let alone the burial? Pretty slim I thought.' Having said that, the prospect of learning something about this important medieval religious house was an exciting one, and Richard agreed to come up with a strategy.

Remarkably, Philippa had captured the imagination of influential people at Leicester City Council and seemed determined to make the project happen – she subsequently commissioned background archaeological research from ULAS in March 2011 and a ground penetrating radar survey of the site in August 2011. She persuaded Leicester City Council and Leicester Shire Promotions to contribute funds for the fieldwork. The University itself then made a very significant financial contribution to the project, working in partnership with Philippa. Richard Buckley proposed the investigation of two trenches in the Social Services car park, with a third to be located when the results of the first two were known. When, in the summer of 2012, it looked as though the project was dead in the water due to a lack of funds, Philippa launched an appeal within the Richard III Society, making up the shortfall within a matter of days. The excavation was on!

The project was launched with a press day on August 24 2012, followed the next day by cutting the tarmac and the machining of the first trench by Mathew Morris down to the level of the archaeology. What happened next took the whole team by surprise – not only was evidence for a human burial revealed in the first few hours of the dig, but the archaeological evidence that emerged during the next ten days showed that it was located within the choir of the Grey Friars church.

The burial was excavated on Wednesday 5 September and had a number of characteristics that led the University of Leicester to announce to the world on the 12 September 2012 that the skeleton of a male with curvature of the spine and evidence for battle wounds had been discovered and therefore had the potential to be Richard III. In the months that followed, the skeleton was subject to painstaking scientific analysis, including radiocarbon dating, investigation of the diet, health,

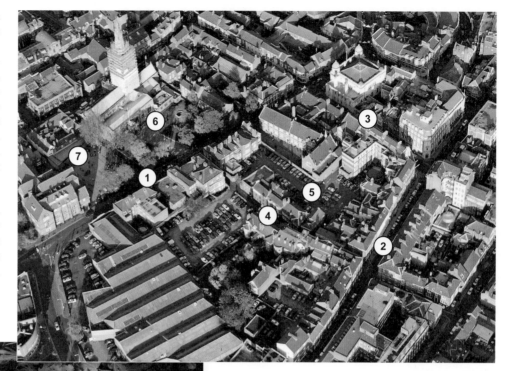

stature and manner of death from detailed examination of the bones and finally analysis of the ancient DNA.

This book tells the story of the archaeological investigation and scientific analysis which led to the momentous announcement by the University of Leicester on February 4 2013, to a room packed with press representatives from all over the world, that 'beyond reasonable doubt, the individual exhumed at Greyfriars in September 2012 is indeed Richard III, the last Plantagenet king of England.'

Above: Aerial view of the Greyfriars site, looking north-east. (1) Peacock Lane; (2) Friar Lane; (3) Grey Friars; (4) New Street; (5) Social Services car park; (6) St Martin's Cathedral; (7) Guildhall.

Left: Launching the project on August 24 2012 (from left to right) Richard Buckley, Annette Carson, Philippa Langley, Michael Ibsen, Turi King and John Ashdown-Hill.

RICARDVS · III · ANG · REX ·

King Richard III

Today, Richard III is perhaps England's most notorious medieval king; immortalised by Shakespeare and others as a schemer responsible for the deaths of Henry VI and his own brother George, Duke of Clarence, and as an evil tyrant and crippled villain who usurped the throne and murdered his own nephews (the Princes in the Tower). Shakespeare weaves a compelling portrait of the king, yet in life he was a loyal brother and a fearless leader who inspired great loyalty amongst his followers, and a lawmaker whose legal reforms still affect us today. It was Richard III who introduced the system of bail as well as commanding that laws be written in English instead of Latin so that they could be understood by everyone. This very polarised image means that he has remained a highly controversial figure of both history and drama ever since his death. Even today he still has a strong cohort of supporters who argue passionately on his behalf.

Richard was born at Fotheringhay Castle in Northamptonshire on 2 October 1452. Fotheringhay had been the principal seat of the House of York since the 14th century and would be Richard's main home for the next seven years. Richard was the seventh and youngest child of Richard, Duke of York and Lady Cecily Neville to survive infancy. His older siblings were Anne (b. 1439), Edward (b. 1440), Edmund (b. 1442), Elizabeth (b. 1444), Margaret (b. 1446) and George (1449). As the youngest child, no-one would have supposed that Richard would one day become the head of his family, even less king of England.

However, Richard grew up in turbulent times. Between 1459 and 1461, the young boy found himself at times a hostage, mourning the loss of his father and brother Edmund (both killed in 1460), then in exile, before his brother Edward finally deposed Henry VI and ascended the throne of England in 1461. Suddenly Richard, just nine years old, found himself not only the Duke of Gloucester but also the brother of King Edward IV and second in line to the throne.

In 1465 Richard, now aged thirteen, entered the household of his cousin Richard Neville, Earl of Warwick, to complete his education, learning the skills required of a successful soldier and statesman. Much of this time was spent at Middleham in Yorkshire.

After his sixteenth birthday, Richard began to play a more prominent role at court. But trouble was again stirring. Both Richard's mentor Warwick and his brother George, Duke of Clarence, were disillusioned with Edward IV's rule. In 1469 they rebelled, but Richard remained faithful to Edward. The following year Warwick and Clarence, with French backing, successfully restored Henry

Left: Richard III by an unknown artist; oil on panel, late 16th century.
NPG148 © National Portrait Gallery, London.

VI to the throne, but in 1471 Edward IV defeated and killed Warwick at the Battle of Barnet and defeated the Lancastrians at Tewkesbury.

Richard fought in both battles. At Barnet he was apparently in the thick of the fighting, losing two close companions and being slightly wounded himself; at Tewkesbury he led the vanguard of his brother's army, again in the centre of the battle. In the aftermath of the fighting – with Warwick dead, the House of Lancaster defeated and Clarence disgraced – Richard emerged as one of the leading noblemen. Edward IV rewarded him with Warwick's northern lands, including Middleham, and made him chief steward of the Duchy of Lancaster lands in the north. Richard married Warwick's daughter Anne, the widow of Edward, son of Henry VI; their only child was a son, Edward of Middleham. The marriage brought Richard into conflict with Clarence again, who was married to Anne's elder sister Isabel. Clarence had assumed he would inherit his father-in-law's lands and title as reward for switching back to Edward IV's side and resented having to share them with his younger brother. The brothers' dispute rumbled on for several years until Clarence's death.

Richard governed the unruly northern counties on behalf of his brother Edward IV, but nevertheless continued to play an important role at court in London as well as having personal interests in Wales and East Anglia. When in 1475 Edward IV invaded France in retaliation for French support of Henry VI, Richard again supported his brother.

In the summer of 1476, Richard officiated over the reburial of his father and his brother Edmund, both hastily buried at Pontefract Abbey in 1460. A lavish ceremonial funeral reunited the three surviving brothers at Fotheringhay, but Clarence's old resentments towards Edward IV and jealousy of Richard's success had not waned. Finally, in 1478, Edward IV could tolerate Clarence's insubordination no longer and he was arrested, tried and executed. Meanwhile, Richard continued successfully to govern the north, showing a knack for dispensing justice fairly and inspiring great loyalty upon which he would come to rely once he was king.

At the end of Edward IV's reign, war with Scotland resumed. In 1482, an English army led by Richard invaded Scotland, capturing the towns of Berwick and Edinburgh before returning to England. The king did not join the campaign in person, trusting in Richard's leadership; he was ailing and died after a short illness on 9 April 1483. This caught everyone by surprise. Richard was still in the north, whilst Edward IV's heir, twelve-year-old Edward, Prince of Wales was at Ludlow in Shropshire, in the care of his maternal uncle Anthony Woodville, Earl Rivers.

The Woodvilles were a minor English family who rose to prominence when Edward IV married Elizabeth Woodville in 1464. Widely resented in England for their rapid rise to power, by the time Edward IV died they controlled much of the royal court, and it looked certain that they would dominate the life of the young Edward V. This worried some on the royal council but events soon overtook their concerns. *En route* for the capital, Richard took charge of his nephew, arresting Rivers and other members of the prince's circle; when Richard and the prince entered London on 4 May, he immediately assumed the protectorship of the realm.

During the following month preparations were made for Edward V's coronation but on 13 June Edward IV's old friend and supporter William, Lord Hastings was seized and summarily executed at the Tower of London amid claims he was conspiring with the Woodvilles against Richard. On 16 June the Archbishop of Canterbury persuaded Elizabeth Woodville to hand over her second son, Richard, Duke of York, so he could attend his brother's coronation; the two princes were housed in the royal apartments at the Tower of London for their comfort and security. With both nephews under his control, Richard postponed the coronation until November. Events then moved rapidly. Richard's claim to the throne was publicised in a sermon in London on 22 June. It was asserted not only that Edward IV was illegitimate, but also that his sons were illegitimate, on the grounds that Edward had a pre-contract of marriage to another woman before he wed Elizabeth Woodville. Richard assumed the throne on 26 June, and was crowned ten days later in a lavish ceremony at Westminster Abbey.

Richard III's reign was short, lasting just over two years. After his coronation he toured the realm, culminating in a triumphant entry into York on 29 August. Meanwhile, the Princes in the Tower disappeared from sight and contemporaries came to believe that they were dead. Opposition to Richard, led by the previously loyal Duke of Buckingham, coalesced around Henry Tudor, the Lancastrian claimant to the throne. Buckingham was soon executed, but sporadic unrest persisted across southern England.

In 1484 Richard called his first and only parliament, during which his rule was ratified and he introduced various reforms to the legal system. But he also suffered personal tragedy when his son and heir, Edward, died, followed soon afterwards by his wife Anne. By now the king was increasingly reliant on a small group of associates against growing opposition to his rule. With the threat of insurrection overshadowing his reign, Richard appears to have welcomed Henry Tudor's return to England, reasoning that defeating him would resolve many of his problems (*see page 16*). Finally, in 1485 the long-awaited invasion occurred and Richard successfully forced a confrontation with the rebels near the town of Market Bosworth in Leicestershire (*see page 20*). However, despite outnumbering Henry's side, Richard lost the battle, being killed in the process, leaving Henry victorious as King Henry VII.

Leicester in Richard III's time

Although there is little left above ground today to remind us, Leicester is an ancient city. Occupation dates back to the late 1st century BC, when the Iron Age peoples known as the Corieltavi established a high-status settlement on the east bank of the River Soar. Leicester grew rapidly following the Roman Conquest in AD 43 and only a hundred years later, the town had a planned layout with public buildings including a forum and baths, and was later provided with first earthen then stone defences. Following the Roman withdrawal from Britain in AD 410, areas both inside and outside the town walls were occupied by the Anglo-Saxons. Leicester was the seat of a Mercian bishop in the 7th–9th centuries, but we know little about the nature of the settlement. In the 9th–10th centuries, Leicester was one of the five boroughs of the Danelaw and it grew to become a town with six churches, 322 houses and a population of about 1500–2000 at the time of the Norman Conquest in 1066.

A castle (**1**) was established in about 1068 at the south-west angle of the ancient Roman walls (**2**), which continued to influence the topography of the medieval borough. The 12th century saw a development boom, with the construction of the stone buildings of the castle, the establishment of Leicester Abbey, the rebuilding of many churches and the expansion of domestic settlement within the walls. More religious houses were established in the 13th century – the Dominicans or Black Friars (**3**) in the north-west corner of the walls, the Augustinian friars (**4**) outside the west gate, on an island between two arms of the river, and the Franciscans, or Grey Friars (**5**) in the southern part of the town, near the Saturday market (**6**).

The 14th century was a period of contrasts. On the one hand the town's population and economy declined; this apparently began during the first decades of the century but was exacerbated by the Black Death in 1348, and resulted in large uninhabited areas within the walls (**7**). On the other hand, Leicester was moving beyond being a small provincial town. By the end of the century, Leicester had become the main centre for the vast Lancastrian estates in the Midlands, administered from the castle in the south-western quarter. Here the earls, later dukes, of Lancaster also established an extra-mural religious precinct known as the Newarke (**8**). The town's importance on the national stage is demonstrated by the number of royal visits it received. Between 1327 and 1345 Edward III stayed there twelve times. Richard II also visited, most notably in 1390 for an extended royal family gathering hosted by his uncle John of Gaunt, Duke of Lancaster.

Left: A bird's-eye view of medieval Leicester from the north-east, as is may have looked in about AD 1450, by Mike Codd.

In 1399, with the accession of Henry IV, the dukes of Lancaster were now kings of England. Whilst Leicester's castle probably fell into decline as a result (*see page 12*), there was a major building programme at the Newarke during the first quarter of the 15th century and the church there effectively became a Lancastrian mausoleum (*see page 13*). Leicester remained important through the 15th century and continued to be a venue for national events, hosting important parliaments in 1414, 1426 and 1450. At the 1426 parliament, King Henry VI was knighted in a lavish ceremony in St Mary de Castro (**9**), alongside the young Richard, Duke of York (Richard III's father).

Despite its longstanding Lancastrian connections, in the mid 15th century the town sided with the House of York, loyally supporting it through the Wars of the Roses. Henry VI was in Leicester in 1450 when a popular revolt led by Jack Cade swept through south-east England and seized London. The town was included in a general pardon issued two years later during a brief reconciliation between Henry VI and the Duke of York. Forces from Leicester supported Edward, Earl of March (later Edward IV) at Towton in 1461, despite many in the county fighting for the Lancastrian cause.

In 1462, when Edward was in Leicester, the town was in high favour with him, and the Borough Records show that he granted an annuity of twenty marks for twenty years 'in consideration of the good and faithful and unpaid service which the mayor and burgesses… have cheerfully rendered of late in our behalf against our enemies… as also of their no small losses incurred touching our business'. Although he subsequently revoked many similar grants to other towns, a special exemption was made for Leicester, and further favour was shown in the grant of an annual fair and another annuity in 1473 for service during the battles of Barnet and Tewkesbury. By this time, much of the county also supported York and in 1471 William, Lord Hastings raised a force of 3000 men from the town and surrounding area to fight for Edward IV.

Richard III also visited the town often, both as a boy and as Duke of Gloucester. When king, he stayed in Leicester at least three times, twice in 1483 and once in 1485. He may also have visited twice in 1484. Little remains above ground of the medieval town that Richard III would have known, but archaeological work around the city is gradually providing more and more information on what it would have looked like. Sites associated with the king include the castle, the Abbey, the Newarke, the Blue Boar Inn and Grey Friars.

Leicester Castle

Leicester Castle was established in about 1068 by Hugh de Grentmaisnil, who built a motte and bailey castle at the south-west angle of the surviving Roman town walls. The motte was a large mound encircled by a ditch, with a timber tower and palisade on top. The bailey was an adjacent enclosure defended by a ditch and rampart, and would have contained a timber hall, stables, a chapel and various other buildings. In the early 12th century, Robert de Beaumont, first Earl of Leicester is thought to have replaced the timber defences with stone and also founded the church of St Mary de Castro in the bailey.

In about 1150, his son Robert 'le Bossu' (the hunchbacked), the second Earl, built the Great Hall, a large rectangular stone building divided into a nave and two aisles – rather like a church – by two rows of tall oak posts linked by great semi-circular timber arches. At the north end of the hall was a platform or dais, where the lord and important retainers would have sat, and in the centre of the building was a large open hearth, the smoke from it drifting upwards through a louvre in the roof. Doors at the south end led to a kitchen block, which was detached from the hall to prevent the spread of fire. Also in this area were rooms for the storage of wine and food, together with a scullery and a bakehouse.

The hall was initially a multi-purpose building: for sleeping, feasting, justice and the administration of the earl's estates. Later, the lord and his family had private apartments at the north end of the hall. These would have included the great chamber with sleeping accommodation and the great dancing chamber, first recorded in the late 14th century, which was the focal point of the range and the scene of music, dancing and merry-making. Documents also refer to other rooms such as the king's chamber, the queen's chamber, the prince's chamber and the wardrobe.

By the 14th century Leicester Castle was becoming central to Lancastrian interests in the Midlands. Thomas, Earl of Lancaster invested heavily in renovating it and his successors spent much time there. During the latter half of the century, the castle was a favoured residence of John of Gaunt (the fourth son of Edward III), but after his death in 1399, his son Henry Bolingbroke, Duke of Lancaster ascended the throne as Henry IV following the deposition of Richard II. Leicester Castle then became just one of many royal residences and probably began to decline in importance. Nevertheless there seems to have been a flurry of building works in the first two decades of the 15th century, with the construction of the Turret Gateway dividing the castle from the Newarke (*see page 13*), and remodelling of the kitchen block to the south of the Great Hall with the addition of a vault and polygonal turrets to the undercroft known as John of Gaunt's Cellar.

In the middle of the 15th century, following a fire, the main gateway to the castle yard and very possibly many of the private domestic apartments were rebuilt, probably at a reduced scale. There was now a timber-framed gatehouse with an adjoining two-storey range above cellars – this survives today as the Judge's Lodgings, a building which is not dissimilar in style to the broadly contemporary Blue Boar Inn (*see page 18*).

In the time of Richard III, the castle contained many more buildings than survive today. We know that he stayed here twice during the first year of his reign, as two letters of 18 August 1483 are signed by him 'from my castle at Leicester' (the second visit was in October that year). This is the last record of the occupation of the castle by a member of the royal family. Richard would almost certainly have held court in the Great Hall, sitting in a prime position on the dais at the north end of this great aisled building – already over 300 years old and very possibly in a poor state of repair judging by later accounts.

Left: Goddard's painting of the interior of the Great Hall in 1821.

The Newarke

In 1330 Henry, Earl of Lancaster and Leicester founded a hospital (later known as Trinity Hospital) to the south of the castle to care for fifty poor and infirm people. The beds were in a long stone building divided into aisles by a series of arches, with little privacy. At one end was a chapel – still surviving today as part of Trinity House – which was used for daily services and to house those residents who were thought likely to recover. Nearby were houses for the master, four chaplains and for five women who tended the sick.

Later in the 14th century, Henry's son – the wealthy Henry Grosmont, Duke of Lancaster – enlarged his father's foundation with the creation of his 'New Work' (*above*), the College of the Annunciation of the Blessed Virgin Mary, which occupied a large precinct on the south side of the castle, later becoming known as the 'The Newarke' (today beneath the campus of De Montfort University). As well as the much enlarged hospital, the college also had a church, a cloister, houses to accommodate a dean and twelve canons (each of whom shared his dwelling with a vicar), houses for the provost and choristers, and a vicars' hall. The ground floor of the Dean's house still survives opposite Trinity House. We have little information on the appearance or layout of most of the college buildings, but it is likely that they were arranged around a series of courtyards in a similar manner to other religious houses. Construction work continued throughout the 14th century, as shown by records of payments for 'completing the church, cloister, houses, walls and other necessary things'.

The church seems to have been finished by about 1414. The poet and antiquary John Leland, who visited Leicester some time before 1542, described it as 'not very great but it is exceeding fair'; he also refers to the many monuments to

Right: The Newarke Gateway today, popularly called The Magazine as a result of being used for the storage of arms in the 17th and 18th centuries.

prominent Lancastrians in the church, including that of Henry, first Duke of Lancaster and his wife Isabella, and the marble tomb of Constance, the wife of John of Gaunt, in front of the high altar. A tomb said to be from the collegiate church survives in the chapel of Trinity Hospital and bears an effigy thought to be of Dame Mary Harvey, a benefactor. All that remains of the church itself are two stone arches, now reconstructed in the basement of De Montfort University's Hawthorn Building.

Further building work in the first quarter of the 15th century saw the Newarke precinct enclosed by a substantial stone wall with a monumental entrance on the east side known as the 'Newarke Gateway' (built about 1400); there was a small gateway on the south side (now demolished) to Mill Lane and later the Turret Gateway provided access into the castle. Three chantry houses were also constructed.

Despite the Newarke's strong Lancastrian connections, after Henry VI had been deposed, the Yorkist kings continued to provide royal patronage for the college. Both Edward IV and Richard III acted on the college's behalf and in 1483 Richard III referred to them as 'our trusty and well-beloved the dean and canons of our new collegiate church of our Blessed Lady of Leicester.' Richard III's final connection with the Newarke came after his death (*see page 22*).

John Curtis 2005

14

Leicester Abbey

Leicester Abbey lay just to the north-east of the medieval borough, beside the main route leading to Nottingham and Derby, in a pleasant spot next to the River Soar. It was founded in 1138–9 as an abbey of Augustinian canons by Robert 'le Bossu', the second Earl of Leicester. To the abbey, Earl Robert transferred the lands that his father had used to endow a college of twelve secular canons at St Mary de Castro within the bailey of Leicester Castle. The abbey was also granted all of the other churches in Leicester, together with a number in Leicestershire and further afield including West Ilsey in Berkshire. On his death in 1168, Robert was buried on the right hand side of the high altar and the earldom passed to his son Robert 'Blanchmains' (white hands), whose devout wife is said to have plaited a long cord from her hair from which to suspend one of the lamps in the choir of the church.

Leicester Abbey grew to become one of the wealthiest religious houses in the country, with a community of canons under the charge of an abbot, who followed a common rule governing the way that they lived. The abbey precinct was enclosed by a substantial wall with a gatehouse on the north side. Like Leicester's friaries, the abbey was dissolved in 1538 and demolished soon afterwards. In the later 16th century, the Hastings family converted the gatehouse into a mansion; this was enlarged by the next owners, the Cavendishes, in the early 17th century, before being burnt down in 1645, during the Civil War.

Apart from the precinct walls, all trace of the abbey had disappeared by the 18th century and it was only in the 19th and 20th centuries that the plans of the principal buildings were revealed through archaeological excavation. In common with other similar establishments, the church lay to the north of a series of buildings that were arranged around a courtyard known as the cloister garth and accessed via covered walkways. On the east side was the chapter house, and above it, at first floor level, the dormitory, which had direct access down a staircase into the church so the canons could attend services during the night. On the south side was the refectory, beyond which was the kitchen, detached from the main buildings to prevent the spread of fire.

The kitchen was investigated by the University of Leicester in 2002–5 and found to be a large square building with corner fireplaces, making the interior octagonal in shape. At nearly 12 metres across internally, it was one of the largest monastic kitchens in the country.

There were further courtyards to the south of the main ranges of buildings, with guest accommodation, an infirmary and lodgings for pensioners ('corrodians'). A survey of the abbey shortly before it was dissolved gives the impression of a large number of buildings in a variety of styles and building materials, reflecting the fact that it had grown piecemeal over a period of 400 years.

Hospitality was an important part of monastic life, and the abbey would be expected to extend a warm welcome to visitors. They would normally be accommodated in the abbey's guest hall or, in special cases, in the abbot's private apartments. Located on a principal route to London from the north, many important travellers passing through the town were entertained at Leicester Abbey during its long history. These included several monarchs, such as Edward III (who, during his visit, famously pardoned a criminal who revived after being hanged), Richard II and his Queen and, on 31 July 1484, Richard III. Senior members of the clergy also stayed here, the most famous of whom was Cardinal Wolsey, who died at the abbey whilst breaking his journey to London to face King Henry VIII in 1530; he was subsequently buried in the Lady Chapel of the abbey church.

On 19 August 1485, Richard III left Nottingham and arrived in Leicester at sunset, almost certainly riding past Leicester Abbey, then down Abbey Gate, entering the town through the North Gate.

Above: A section of in situ medieval tile floor excavated in Leicester Abbey's eastern cloister walk in 2008.

Left: A reconstruction drawing of Leicester Abbey in its heyday, by John Finnie.

The road to Bosworth Field

The Battle of Bosworth, fought on 22 August 1485, was the final act of a bloody civil war that had been waged sporadically for 30 years by rival branches of the royal family, the Plantagenets, for control of the English throne. Today this conflict is known as the Wars of the Roses in reference to the heraldic badges of the two families – the white rose of York and the red rose of Lancaster. A romantic but apocryphal event is portrayed in Shakespeare's play *Henry VI Part 1*, when arguing supporters of the rival factions pick different colour roses in a garden to show their allegiance.

In 1471 the Lancastrians suffered a catastrophic defeat at the Battle of Tewkesbury, when most of their leadership was killed, including Edward Prince of Wales, the heir to the throne. King Henry VI himself died shortly afterwards at the Tower of London. For the next twelve years the House of York, in the person of Edward IV, ruled England peacefully and the war appeared to be over. However, when Richard III seized the throne from the young Edward V in 1483, old Lancastrian sympathies re-emerged, coalescing around the senior remaining Lancastrian claimant to the throne, Henry Tudor, Earl of Richmond (on his mother's side he was the great-great-great-grandson of Edward III and the great-great-grandson of John of Gaunt, Duke of Lancaster).

Henry had been in exile in France for fourteen years but after Richard III's accession to the throne his supporters encouraged him to pursue his own claim. Following one failed attempt in 1483, when his invasion fleet was forced to turn back due to bad weather, Henry Tudor successfully landed at Milford Haven in Wales on 7 August 1485 with a small army of English exiles and French mercenaries. As he marched through Wales he was joined by both Welshmen and more English defectors, and when he crossed the English border and arrived at Shrewsbury in Shropshire on 16 August his army numbered some 5000 troops.

From Shrewsbury, Henry advanced through the Midlands along Watling Street (today the A5) towards London, reaching Atherstone in Warwickshire, on the border with Leicestershire, on 21 August. Here he probably hoped to rendezvous with troops from north Wales and the north-west commanded by his stepfather, Lord Stanley, but Stanley refused to commit himself, choosing to stay neutral until circumstances favoured him better.

Meanwhile, Richard III, aware of impending invasion since June, had positioned himself in Nottingham, a central location from which he could react swiftly to a threat from any corner of his realm. News of Henry's invasion reached him there on 11 August and he immediately summoned his supporters, ordering his southern and East Anglian contingents to meet him in Leicester, whilst he waited in Nottingham for his northern forces, including those of the Stanley family. Lord Stanley, however, replied that he was sick, an ambivalence which alarmed Richard III, who took Stanley's son hostage to ensure his co-operation.

Leaving Nottingham with his army, Richard III reached Leicester just before sunset on 19 or 20 August. The chronicler Edward Hall, writing in 1542, describes his arrival: 'Then he [Richard III] with a frowning countenance and truculent aspect mounted on a great white courser [horse]… with great pomp entered the town of Leicester after the sun set.' Although it was not recorded, his army presumably camped outside the town, perhaps in the fields around the abbey, whilst Richard himself is said to have stayed at the Blue Boar Inn.

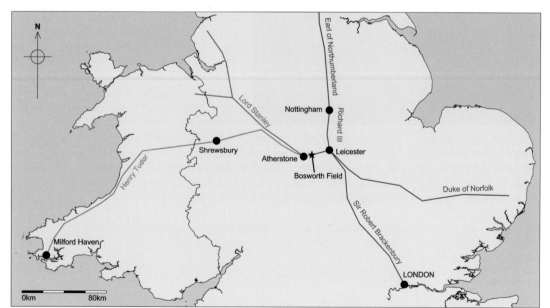

Left: The routes of the opposing armies: Richard III's (blue), Henry Tudor's (red) and Lord Stanley's (green). After Foard & Curry 2013.

Richard III's arrival in Leicester

Blue Boar Inn
In 1485, Richard III is said to have spent the nights of 19 and 20 August here (*see page 18*).

The North Gate
The North Gate stood on the site of its Roman predecessor and may have incorporated some of the original Roman masonry. All four of Leicester's gates were notoriously low and narrow and it was reported that 'a foot passenger meeting a carriage went in danger of his life.' Richard III may have had to duck or dismount before he entered the town. The gate was demolished in 1774.

St Johns' Hospital
The Hospital of St John the Evangelist and St John the Baptist was Leicester's first hospital, built before the 13th century. By the 14th century its role was largely superseded by Trinity Hospital in the Newarke (*see page 13*) but parts of its chapel survived into the 18th century and a hospice bearing its name remained on the site until the mid 20th century. Next to it were the County Jail and the Shire Hall.

All Saints Church
One of Leicester's oldest churches, most probably a late Saxon foundation, but extensively rebuilt in the 12th, 14th and 15th centuries. It occupies a prominent position on the medieval High Street, from which it could be entered through its Norman west door.

Medieval inn
Parts of this medieval timber-framed building with three gables survive today in No. 107 Highcross Street. Tree-ring dating shows that the inn was built in the 14th century. It would have been one of the first buildings Richard III saw when he entered the town. By the 16th century it was known as the Cross Keys Inn.

The north suburb
From Nottingham, Richard III would have ridden through the northern suburb – where the dyers and fullers occupied land next to the river – and entered Leicester through the North Gate.

The Blue Boar Inn

Having reached Leicester, Richard III by tradition stayed at the Blue Boar Inn. This elaborate timber-framed building was located on the medieval High Street (now Highcross Street), appropriately close to where a Travelodge stands today. Although it may seem odd that he was not accommodated at the castle, this may be because it was either unprepared or had insufficient room for the king and his large retinue. It would not be especially unusual for a king to stay at a local inn at that time; they were quality establishments, which provided food, lodgings and stabling for travellers, including wealthy merchants, aristocrats and royalty. In many respects medieval inns were the grand hotels of their day. Some were built as an investment by corporations, such as a college or a monastery, requiring considerable financial investment, but with the guarantee of a good steady income for years to come.

Typically, inns would have buildings on the street frontage and a gateway providing access to a rear courtyard that might be surrounded by further ranges, with first-floor accommodation accessed via external staircases and galleries. The chambers housing the guests were usually quite large, as much as 6.1m (20ft) by 3.7–4.6m (12–15ft), with room for several beds, accommodating at least four people. It is likely that there were also garderobes (toilets) at first-floor level. On the ground floor, there would usually be a large hall where guests ate and drank, a kitchen, stables and a buttery and pantry for storing wine, bread and provisions.

There are few historical references to the Blue Boar Inn and even its name in the 15th century is uncertain. Some believe that it was originally called the White Boar (Richard III's emblem), the sign being torn down after Bosworth and the name hastily changed to Blue Boar (the insignia of Henry VII's general, John, Earl of Oxford). Later, there are hints that it changed its name again to the Blue Bell, although this may simply be confusion with another Leicester inn.

The Blue Boar was demolished in March 1836; the wing that by tradition housed Richard III was recorded in a number of early 19th-century engravings, the most well-known of which were by the noted local artist, John Flower. A Leicester architect, Henry Goddard, also made a detailed record of the building before the timber frame was dismantled, with meticulous drawings including the roof structure, timber joints and mouldings, all carefully annotated with measurements.

It is thought that the part of the inn that remained in the 19th century was just one wing of a much larger structure, perhaps originally with two wings on either side of a gatehouse that provided access to a rear courtyard. The ground

Above: A 19th-century lithograph of the Blue Boar Inn in Highcross Street, by Leicester artist John Flower.

floor of the surviving wing was one large room (41ft long and 24ft wide), with a substantial stone fireplace, windows (but no door) to the street elevation and a window to the rear that would have looked onto the courtyard.

The first-floor chamber – said to have been occupied by Richard III – overhung the lower storey (a 'jetty') and had a projecting oriel window overlooking the street and a large gable with ornamental timber barge boards. This chamber also had a large stone fireplace and was open to the rafters. Inside, the timbers were apparently decorated with painted scrollwork in black, red and yellow. Access to the chamber is thought to have been via an oak-planked door from an external gallery at first-floor level off the courtyard.

Richard III leaves Leicester

Richard III rode out from Leicester on Sunday 21 August. A chronicler writing in 1486 describes his departure: 'the king proceeded on his way, amid the greatest pomp, and wearing the crown on his head; being attended by John Howard, Duke of Norfolk, and Henry Percy, Earl of Northumberland, and other mighty lords, knights and esquires, together with a countless multitude of the common people.'

West Bridge
Richard III would have first ridden across West Bridge, over the eastern arm of the Soar. This bridge was originally built in the 11th century but was extensively rebuilt in the 14th century when a small chapel of Our Lady of the Bridge was built over its eastern arch.

The Bow Bridges
Two bridges crossed the western arm of the Soar near the Augustinian friary. Bow Bridge carried the road to Hinckley, whilst the smaller Little Bow Bridge gave the friars access to a close containing St Augustine's Well. *See page 28* for the legends concerning 'King Richard's Bridge'.

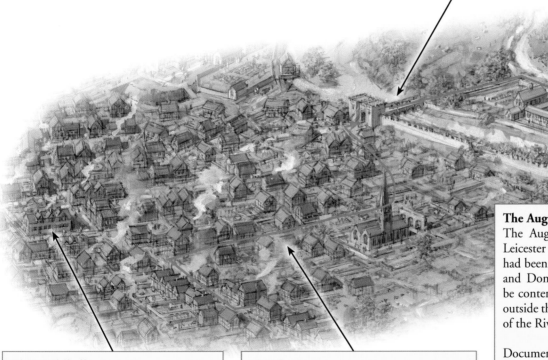

The Guildhall
The guildhall was built in about 1390 as the meeting place of the Guild of Corpus Christi, the leading medieval guild in Leicester. Guilds were associations of craftsmen and merchants. In the late 15th century the Borough Corporation began using the building as a town hall.

Hot Gate
On leaving the Blue Boar Inn, Richard III probably rode along the High Street to the High Cross before turning west onto Hot Gate, so called because the town's public bread ovens were located nearby. As it neared the river this street was known as Apple Gate, perhaps because of surrounding orchards.

The Augustinian Friary
The Augustinian (or Austin) Friars were late arrivals in Leicester in 1254, by which time the prime sites in the town had been taken by the other orders of friars, the Franciscans and Dominicans. This perhaps explains why they had to be content with a rather awkward, cramped and damp site outside the walls of the medieval borough, between two arms of the River Soar.

Documents record that the friars had built their church by 1306; excavations in 1973–8 showed that this lay on the south side of the site, next to the main route into Leicester from the west. North of the church were two cloisters separated by a wide drain. The larger southern cloister had the refectory and dormitory ranges on its northern and eastern sides respectively. The smaller cloister had buildings on its western, northern and eastern sides. The friary was dissolved in 1538 and all of its buildings had been demolished by 1542–3.

The Battle of Bosworth

Having gathered his remaining forces in Leicester, which probably numbered 8-10,000 men, Richard III was now perfectly positioned to cut off Henry's march to London along Watling Street. Knowing that Henry was nearing Atherstone, he decided to challenge the rebels, and on 21 August marched out from Leicester, threatening to catch Henry with a flank attack if he did not turn and fight. That night the two armies were just 6 miles apart, with Richard III camped close to Sutton Cheney, possibly on Ambion Hill, and Henry at Atherstone.

Unlike Richard III, Henry had no military experience and although nominally in command himself, his army relied on his experienced general, John de Vere, Earl of Oxford. Both armies comprised infantry, archers and cavalry, but Richard also had field artillery. However, the majority of Richard III's troops were inexperienced levies whilst Henry's were mostly 'professional' mercenaries.

Although heavily outnumbered, the next morning the rebels had no choice but to face the king. As Henry's men advanced they came under fire from Richard III's cannons and Oxford decided to attack the right flank of the royal army which was under the command of John Howard, Duke of Norfolk, rather than risk a frontal assault. Drawing his men up in a tight wedge, protected on one side by a marsh, Oxford was able to break through Norfolk's formation and during the fierce fighting Norfolk was killed.

Seeing that Norfolk's men were losing and that his rear-guard commanded by Henry Percy, Earl of Northumberland would or could not engage the enemy, Richard III risked a daring move that could have won him the battle if it had succeeded. Seeing Henry isolated from his main forces, protected only by a small group of men, the king and his mounted knights charged in an attempt to kill the rebel leader. Richard's men broke through Henry's bodyguard, getting close enough to Henry to kill his standard bearer, but now the forces led by Sir William Stanley finally committed themselves, coming to Henry's aid in a decisive counter-attack. Outnumbered and outmanoeuvred, Richard was cut off from his own bodyguard and killed.

With Richard dead, the royal army fled, hotly pursued by the victorious rebels. In the aftermath of the battle, Richard's crown was said to have been found in a thorn bush on Crown Hill near Stoke Golding and was used to crown Henry Tudor, King Henry VII.

Left: Medieval re-enactors recreate the Battle of Bosworth during the 2012 Anniversary Weekend at the Bosworth Battlefield Heritage Centre.

Finding the real battlefield: The Bosworth Battlefield Survey

Considering the significance of the Battle of Bosworth, it is perhaps surprising that for the last 500 years no-one has really known exactly where it was fought. The few contemporary records give conflicting accounts and many of the place-names mentioned do not survive on any maps. Broad consensus is that the battle was fought between the villages of Sutton Cheney, Shenton, Dadlington and Stoke Golding, some 13 miles south-west of Leicester. For much of the last 200 years it was widely believed that the battle was fought on a local landmark, Ambion Hill. However, more recently there has been much debate as to the true location of the battlefield, with various contending sites.

In 2005 the Battlefields Trust, on behalf of Leicestershire County Council, began a major new historical, topographical and archaeological survey of the battlefield. After four years of intense work, the team of specialists and volunteers were able to identify an area where at least a substantial part of the battle took place, approximately 2 miles south-west of Ambion Hill, alongside the route leading south-west from Leicester towards Atherstone, which followed the old Roman road to Mancetter and Watling Street (Fenn Lane). Historical research on the battle and a reconstruction of the medieval landscape by mapping place-names and carrying out soil and pollen analysis narrowed the search down and provided evidence for the marsh in which Richard III's horse was said to have fallen (Fenn Hole).

In 2009 an archaeological survey with metal detectors finally located the battlefield. Over 30 lead round shot of different sizes fired from early field guns were recovered – the largest number ever found

Silver gilt boar badge (actual size 35mm) found at Bosworth battlefield.

on a European medieval battlefield. These results have changed the way historians view the role of cannon in late medieval battles.

Very few other objects that might be related to the battle were discovered, apart from the guard from a late 15th century sword; perhaps surprisingly no arrowheads have yet been found. No doubt as much as possible would have been recovered or scavenged after the fighting was over.

One iconic item – the Bosworth Boar (*above*) – was, however, found amongst the battlefield debris, close to the medieval marsh of Fenn Hole. A white boar was the king's personal emblem and this little silver gilt badge would have been made for Richard III's coronation. It was almost certainly lost by one of his knights during the battle; indeed the discovery of the badge is a vital clue in helping locate the battle site.

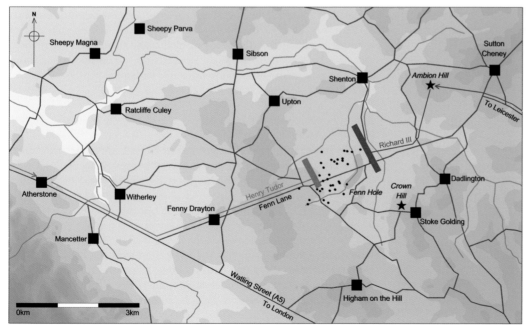

Left: The Battle of Bosworth in its new location, showing the approach routes of the armies of Richard III and Henry Tudor, and the distribution of round shot found on the battlefield (black dots). After Foard & Curry 2013.

Buried 'without any pompe or solemne funeral...'

So what happened to Richard's corpse after he was killed at Bosworth? An account of about 1486 says that 'Richard's body was found among the other slain… many other insults were heaped on it, and, not very humanely, a halter was thrown round the neck, and it was carried to Leicester.' It seems that this was done with little respect, and a Castilian report of early 1486 mentions that Richard's body was 'covered from the waist downward with a black rag of poor quality, [Earl Henry] ordering him to be exposed there three days to the universal gaze.' A later account of the historian Polydore Vergil refers to the king's body being 'nakyd of all clothing, and layd upon an horse bake with the armes and legges hanginge downe on both sydes'. At about the same date, the Tudor chronicler Robert Fabyan, wrote 'And Richard late King…was… brought into that town, for his body despoiled to the skin, and nought being left about him, so much as would cover his privy member, he was trussed behind a pursuivant [herald] called Norroy as an hog or another vile beast, and all besprung with mire and filth was brought to a church in Leicester for all men to wonder upon…'.

Henry with his victorious army accompanied the body to Leicester where he stayed for two days, during which time William Catesby, one of Richard's principal councillors who fought alongside him at Bosworth, was beheaded. The main reason for Henry to come to Leicester, rather than heading south to London as one might expect, was almost certainly so that he could display the deposed king's body and show the townsfolk that Richard was indeed dead. The people of Leicester were after all the last to have seen him alive before he marched off to meet Henry in battle. Word would soon get around about the death of the king, thereby preventing the appearance of potential imposters who could be the focus for further dissent.

In the Ballad of Bosworth Field, thought to have been written by a Plantagenet supporter within a few years of 1485, we are told:

> they brought King Richard thither with might
> as naked as he borne might bee,
> & in Newarke laid was hee,
> that many a one might looke on him.

This suggests that Richard's naked body was displayed in the Newarke, perhaps in the church of the Annunciation of the Blessed Virgin Mary with its many tombs of prominent Lancastrians – a final insult to the memory of the defeated Yorkist. This is not absolutely certain, however, and he may have been taken directly to the church of the Franciscan Friars and exhibited there, before being buried two days later. The late 15th-century historian and antiquary John Rous records that 'at last [Richard] was buried in the choir of the Friars Minor at Leicester', whilst Polydore Vergil early in the 16th century says that Richard was 'brought to the Franciscan monastery at Leicester, a sorry spectacle but a sight worthy of the man's life, and there it was given burial two days later, without the usual funeral rites' (or in early translations 'without any pompe or solemne funeral'). Richard was probably buried on 25 August, the day Henry left Leicester for London.

Burying deposed monarchs in religious houses away from the political hub of London had precedent. Eighty-five years earlier, Richard II was initially buried in the Dominican friary at Kings Langley (Hertfordshire) before Henry V had him reburied in Westminster Abbey. Friaries were also commonly chosen as resting places for the executed dead, if they were of high standing. We can never know whether Henry ordered the interment of Richard III in the church of Leicester's Franciscan friary or whether the friars themselves took the initiative – perhaps because they had Yorkist sympathies. However, the fact that all the evidence points to a rather hasty burial suggests that the latter is unlikely and the friars might also have attracted unwanted scrutiny from the victorious Lancastrians. It seems more likely that the order came from Henry VII himself, perhaps because he was a devotee of St Francis, a practice he acquired during his long exile in Brittany, and so he may have favoured the Franciscans to carry out his wishes, or been influenced by Franciscans in his entourage.

Left: Richard's body is brought back to Leicester, illustration by Victor Ambrus.

King Richard's tomb

A decade after Richard III's death, Henry VII decided that a suitable tomb should be placed over his predecessor's grave – a small but symbolic act of reconciliation. Chancery records from 1496 show that in July 1495, Henry VII's royal commissioners arranged for Walter Hylton, a Nottingham alabasterman, to erect a memorial over the grave. He was to receive £50 for the work (£20 up front and the rest on completion), a decent sum of money, but nothing compared to the £1,500 to be spent on Henry VII's own tomb in Westminster Abbey. In September 1495, a royal household account book records another payment of £10 1s to a James Keyley 'for King Richard's tombe'. What actually transpired is somewhat unclear: did Hylton actually carry out the work? Was Keyley working on behalf of Hylton, or was he a sub-contractor? Or did Hylton carve the monument and Keyley install it? Sadly, we do not know.

No detailed descriptions of the tomb survive either but later chroniclers, some of whom may have seen it before it was destroyed, suggest that it bore a carved likeness of Richard III on a coloured alabaster slab. The words of the epitaph do survive (*right*). This appears to have been a bronze plaque, which would have been placed near the tomb. Perhaps surprisingly, as the epitaph can be regarded as the 'official' position of Henry VII's government towards Richard III, the text is not overtly hostile. Had Tudor attitudes towards Richard mellowed, or had sufficient time passed safely to erect a memorial to the dead king?

The timing of the tomb's commissioning, a decade after Richard III's death, is significant. In the early years of Henry's rule, he was forced to contend with a number of Yorkist pretenders to the throne. The first was a young boy called Lambert Simnel, who appeared in Ireland in 1487 claiming to be Edward, Earl of Warwick, the son of George, Duke of Clarence (the brother of Edward IV and Richard III). Simnel was a pawn of a group of Yorkist die-hards led by the Earl of Lincoln (a nephew of Richard III) and supported by Margaret of York, dowager Duchess of Burgundy (Richard's sister). The boy was crowned Edward VI in Dublin, but an invasion of England came to nothing and the rebels were defeated on 16 June 1487 at the Battle of Stoke Field, near Newark in Nottinghamshire.

The second and more serious pretender was a young man called Perkin Warbeck, who claimed in 1491 that he was Richard of Shrewsbury, Duke of York (the younger son of Edward IV; one of the Princes in the Tower). Warbeck too found support from Margaret of York, as well as the Holy Roman Emperor, Maximilian I. In England, old loyalties to the House of York induced some senior members of Henry VII's court to begin plotting on Warbeck's behalf and in July 1495, Warbeck led an unsuccessful invasion of England.

> ## The King's epitaph
>
> *I, here, whom the earth encloses under various coloured marble,*
> *Was justly called Richard the Third.*
> *I was Protector of my country, an uncle ruling on behalf of his nephew.*
> *I held the British kingdom in trust, they were disunited.*
> *Then for just sixty days less two,*
> *And two summers, I held my sceptres.*
> *Fighting bravely in war, deserted by the English,*
> *I succumbed to you, King Henry VII.*
> *But you yourself, piously, at your expense, thus honoured my bones*
> *And caused a former king to be revered with the honour of a king*
> *When twice five years less four**
> *Three hundred five-year periods of our salvation had passed.*
> *And eleven days before the Kalends of September***
> *I surrendered to the red rose the power it desired.*
> *Whoever you are, pray for my offences,*
> *That my punishment may be lessened by your prayers.*
>
> Translated from Latin by John Ashdown-Hill
>
> *This numbers game is a complex way of conveying a date. It calculates as 1494 (2 x 5 = 10; 10 − 4 = 6; 300 x 5 = 1500; 1500 − 6 = 1494). However, as the text implies that this is the date of Richard's death (1485), the writer appears to have become muddled, perhaps accidentally substituting the year in which he was composing the verse.
> ** 22 August.

It is against this backdrop of unrest that Henry VII decided to erect a tomb to Richard III, and it is telling that the date of commission coincides with Warbeck's first invasion attempt. Was it a deliberate effort by Henry VII to appease Yorkist/Lancastrian divisions and unite the country against the pretender?

Henry VII spared Lambert Simnel, making him a servant in the royal household. Warbeck on the other hand remained a threat for several more years. He found a new backer in King James IV of Scotland and took part in two more unsuccessful invasions of England, in 1496 and 1497, before he was eventually caught and imprisoned for life in the Tower of London. In 1499 he became entangled in one last plot, an attempt to free the real Edward, Earl of Warwick from the Tower. This also failed and Warbeck was hanged at Tyburn.

Grey Friars – Leicester's Franciscan friary

Franciscan friars first arrived in Leicester between AD 1224 and 1230, but we do not know exactly when or who founded their friary. Tradition going back to at least the 16th century holds that it was founded by Simon de Montfort II, who became Earl of Leicester in 1238. Although this is unlikely, de Montfort was very probably an early benefactor.

The friary (**1**) occupied a large walled precinct west of Leicester's Saturday market-place (**2**), between two important medieval thoroughfares, Friar Lane (**3**) and St Francis' Lane (**4**) – today known as Peacock Lane – both connecting the town's High Street (**5**) – today Highcross Street – and the South Gate (**6**) with the Saturday market. This was a perfect place for the friars to beg for alms outside the friary on streets which were sure to have a regular flow of traders and passers-by.

The first reference to the friary's church dates to 1255 when Simon de Montfort's wife Eleanor, Countess of Leicester persuaded her brother King Henry III to grant eighteen oak trees to the friars to make '[choir] stalls and for panelling their chapel', implying the near-completion of the choir of the church at this time. The nave of the church, with a north aisle, was completed thirty-five years later in 1290. Other documented buildings include a chapter house, refectory, infirmary and possibly a theology school.

The friary also had large areas of garden within its precinct and a cemetery was situated between the church and St Francis' Lane.

In 1402 the friary became notorious when three of its friars, along with others from the East Midlands were executed for treason along with Sir Roger Clarendon, an illegitimate brother of King Richard II, and Walter Baldock, a former prior of Launde in Leicestershire. They had become caught up in a plot, endorsed by Robert III, King of Scots, to spread seditious rumours through England that King Richard II (d. 1400) was still alive and well and planning on returning to reclaim his throne from King Henry IV.

At trial, the men were twice acquitted before a third jury found them guilty. The condemned friars (a Doctor of Divinity called Roger Frisby, and two brethren called Walter Walton and John Moody) were hanged and beheaded at Tyburn and their heads displayed on London Bridge. Afterwards, their bodies were collected by their brethren and may have been buried in London or taken back to Leicester.

Of those buried in the friary only four are named with any certainty: Peter Swynsfeld, seventh Provincial Minister of the English Franciscans (d. 1272); Emma, wife of John of Holt (d. 1290); William of Nottingham, seventeenth Provincial Minister (d. 1330); and 'a knight called Mutton, sometime mayor of Leicester' – who may be Sir William Moton of Peckleton (d. 1356–62). The unnamed wife of Sir William de Harley may have also been buried in the church. Her funeral feast was certainly held at the friary, to which the town contributed wine, bread and fish.

Little else is known about the early history of this important medieval institution. In 1327 a murderer call John of Busseby sought sanctuary in the church for five weeks before managing to escape (he was later pardoned) and in 1414 King Henry V held a parliament in Leicester, using some of the friary buildings for committee meetings.

Nor do we know how big the friary was. In 1300 at least eighteen friars resided at Leicester and by the mid 14th century there may have been as many as 20–30 friars in the community. In 1349 a Gilbert Lavener and his wife Ellen donated a property in the town to the friars so they could enlarge the friary. However, numbers may have begun to drop after the arrival of the Black Death in 1348 and by the 15th century there may have only been a dozen friars left.

What is a friar?

Friars took the same vows of poverty, chastity and obedience as monks, but they followed a different way of life. Unlike cloistered monks or canons, such as those at Leicester Abbey, their mission was to teach and preach to lay people, and they were visible around the town. Friars were often well educated, compared with parish priests.

There is another important difference. Friars took their vows of poverty fairly seriously; they were 'mendicants,' meaning that they earned their living from begging and accepting payment in return for religious services offered. They did not have estates or other sources of regular revenue, unlike other orders; Leicester Abbey, for example, was very wealthy.

Why are they called Grey Friars?

Franciscan friars – named after their founder, the Italian St Francis of Assisi – were known as Grey Friars because of the colour of their clothing, a gown (habit) of grey cloth and a belt of rope with three knots symbolising their vows. Their official title is the 'Order of Friars Minor'.

Left: Artist's reconstruction of the Grey Friars quarter of medieval Leicester in about 1450, showing a possible layout for the friary buildings. Artwork by Mike Codd.

Dissolution, demolition and development

Little is known about the last fifty-three years of the friary, leading up to its demise during Henry VIII's Dissolution of the Monasteries in the 1530s. However, in 1513 a prominent wool merchant and former Mayor of Leicester called William Wyggeston set up a hospital to care for the poor. He chose a site next to St Martin's church for the building and leased the land from the Grey Friars. Seven years later, the hospital leased a second piece of land from the friars, called St Francis' Garden. We do not know where this garden was located, although it was probably nearby.

On 10 November 1538, the remaining friars surrendered their house to Henry VIII's commissioners, who made an inventory of the friary's assets, sold off everything of value and rendered the buildings uninhabitable. The last seven friars were the warden William Giles, the reader Simon Harvey, and Henry Shepherd, John Stanish, Robert Aston, Radulph Heyrick and William Abbot. At this time they appear to have been very poor, subsisting largely on alms; a record of the friary's annual rental value lists a sum total of just £1 4s, a fraction of the wealth of Leicester Abbey, which was valued at £786 16s 1¾d.

The Grey Friars site was sold for £24 3s 4d in 1545 to John Bellowe and John Broxholme – 16th-century property speculators from Lincolnshire – as part of a large land purchase which also included Leicester's Augustinian friary. In the years that followed the friary appears to have been systematically demolished, with some of its stone and timber being sold to St Martin's church. By the late 16th century Robert Herrick (*right*) had acquired the plot, and on it built a large mansion close to Friar Lane (under the modern street called Grey Friars). The remainder of the land was occupied by gardens. When in 1612, Herrick showed Christopher Wren (father of the famous architect) the site of Richard III's grave, it was 'covered with a handsome Stone Pillar, three Foot high, with this inscription, *Here lies the Body of Richard III. Some Time King of England*'.

Greyfriars House remained in the possession of the Herrick family until 1711, when Robert's great-grandson Samuel Herrick sold it. In the following decades much of the property was divided and sold off. In 1743 New Street was laid through the site and in 1759 a fine new townhouse was built on part of the land. This still survives today at No. 17 Friar Lane (*see page 32*). In 1776 Greyfriars House was sold to Thomas Pares, who in 1800 established the bank Pares & Co. in the north-east corner of its garden. The land was sold on again in 1824 and Herrick's mansion was finally demolished in 1871. A new street, Grey Friars, was laid through the site in 1873 and the remaining land was sold for commercial development. This included the Leicester Trustee Savings Bank, built on the corner of St Martin's and Grey Friars in 1873.

Part of the land at No. 17 Friar Lane was sold in 1863 to the Alderman Newton's Boy's School (*see page 33*) and after 1915 the remaining property was acquired by Leicestershire County Council. Smart new offices were constructed in the 1920s and 1930s, which were used until 1965, when County Hall was opened. Since then, the buildings have been used by Leicester City Council, with the former gardens serving as a staff car park.

Robert Herrick (*above*) came from a prominent family of wealthy ironmongers in Leicester. Born in 1540, just two years after the friary was dissolved, he would have been familiar with the ruins as he grew up. Herrick became a town councillor in 1567, marrying Elizabeth Manby in the same year. He followed in the footsteps of his father and uncle as Mayor of Leicester, holding the position in 1584, 1593 and 1605. He was also a Justice of the Peace, an alderman and MP for Leicester in 1588. Today, Herrick's portrait still hangs in Leicester's medieval guildhall. The Mayoral Roll records *'for some years prior to his death, he resided in a mansion house within the precincts and grounds of the dissolved Grey Friars monastery.'* He died in 1618, aged 78, and was buried in St Martin's church.

The 'King's Bed' and murder most foul

Since Richard III's death, many legends have arisen concerning the king. During the Bosworth campaign in 1485, he is said to have brought his bed with him from Nottingham, which was then set up for him in the Blue Boar Inn. When the king left Leicester, his bed remained behind, perhaps because it was too large to use in the royal tent and because he had every intention of using it again when he returned to Leicester.

This, of course, never happened. After the battle the bed seems to have stayed at the Blue Boar, passing from tenant to tenant. In the early 17th century, it is said that when it was being made up by the landlady, Mrs Clark, a gold coin dropped out. Her curiosity aroused, she carefully examined the bed and, finding it to have a double bottom, she prised off the upper board and found the space to be filled with gold coins, some of Richard III and some earlier. The discovery was kept secret, but the Clarks became wealthy as a result. Mr Clark was subsequently mayor of Leicester; after his death, Mrs Clark continued to keep the inn, but by this time rumours seem to have spread amongst the servants of the treasure in the bedstead.

In autumn 1604, a criminal on the run from Staffordshire, Thomas Harrison, lodged at the inn and, having wooed Mrs Clark's servant, Alice Grimbold, was told by her that a large quantity of money was kept in the house by her mistress. In February the following year, he returned with an accomplice, Edward Bradshaw, and tied up Mrs Clark and her servants before stealing the money from a large coffer in her parlour. During the robbery, Mrs Clark apparently tried to cry out and was murdered, most likely by Bradshaw. The criminals fled, but were quickly apprehended along with a third man, Adam Bonus, who established his innocence and disclosed all he knew about the affair, pleading that Alice Grimbold was the instigator of the plot. Following a trial at Leicester assizes in March 1605, Bradshaw was condemned to hang for his crime, whilst poor Alice – found to be an accomplice in the robbery and murder – received the unnecessarily harsh and cruel sentence to be burnt at the stake.

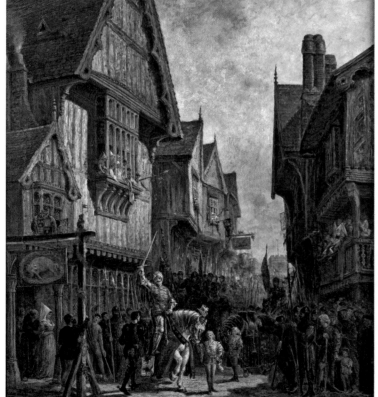

After the murder, the bed became quite famous and in 1611 'King Richards bed-sted i' Leyster' was included on a list of sights and exhibitions in England which could be seen for a penny. Later, the bed was purchased by the Herrick family and was kept for many years at Beaumanor Hall, before finally ending up in the collections of Leicestershire Museums Service, where it is on display at Donington le Heath Manor House. It has long been recognised that the superstructure of the bed does not date from the time of Richard III (it is more likely to be 16th–18th century date, with even later additions), but the rectangular oak base from which the bed ropes are strung could possibly be late medieval.

Above: Engraving of 'King Richard's bed' by Leicester antiquarian John Throsby in 1791.

Left: Richard III outside the Blue Boar Inn in Leicester. Oil on canvas, painted by Leicester-born artist John Fulleylove in 1880.

'King Richard's Bridge' and the 'King's Coffin'

Above: 'King Richard's Bridge', the medieval Bow Bridge in 1861 with the memorial plaque to Richard III mounted on the building to the right. London Illustrated News, 5 February 1861.

'King Richard's Bridge'

'Upon this Bridge … stood a stone of some height, against which King Richard, as he passed toward Bosworth, by chance struck his spur, and against the same stone as he was brought back, hanging by the horse side, his head was dashed and broken, as a wise woman (forsooth) had foretold, who, before Richards going to battle, being asked of his success, said that where his spur struck, his head should be broken'

John Speed, *Historie of Great Britaine*, 1611

The best-known Leicester legends concerning Richard III were first published by the cartographer and antiquarian John Speed in 1611. The origin of the tale of Richard striking his spur against the bridge and the resulting prophecy of the wise/old/mad woman (stories vary) is difficult to track down, but may be a narrative device created to help establish that Richard III, the 'ill-fated', 'evil' usurper and child-murderer, was doomed to fail. Historians in the 16th and 17th centuries often followed the Renaissance tradition of using history to teach moral lessons. However, there could be a germ of truth behind the tale. The carriageway across Bow Bridge was only 6ft wide, enough for only a single waggon to cross at once, originally with niches on both sides to allow people on foot to get out of the way of larger traffic. It is possible then, with crowds of people gathering to watch the pomp and pageantry of Richard III's departure from Leicester on 21 August, and a bridge only wide enough for two horses to cross abreast, that Richard's spur may have brushed against the bridge parapet, the moment being remembered by people in the crowd.

The present Bow Bridge, built in 1862, was designed by the city as a memorial to Richard III. Its decorative ironwork bears the town's coat-of-arms (a white cinquefoil on a red shield) interspersed with roses and the coats-of-arms of Richard III and Henry VII. Richard's arms show his white boar emblem and his motto 'Loyaulte me Lie', meaning 'Loyalty Binds Me.'

The fate of Richard's remains

'His [Richard III's] body… (as tradition hath delivered) was borne out of the City, and contemptuously bestowed under the end of Bow-Bridge, which giveth passage over a branch of Soare upon the west side of the Town.'

John Speed, *Historie of Great Britaine*, 1611

This story, first written down seventy-three years after it allegedly happened, was still commonly believed until the recent discovery of Richard III's remains. It was thought that, during the destruction of the friary, Richard's body was dug up and paraded through the streets of Leicester by a jeering mob, before finally being cast into the River Soar off Bow Bridge. Another version adds that after the mob dispersed a few pitying bystanders pulled the corpse from the water and hastily reburied it in the graveyard of the Augustinian friary next to the bridge. These embellishments have been added to Speed's original story over the last 400 years.

This legend was very popular in the Victorian period and in 1856 a local builder, Benjamin Broadbent, erected a memorial plaque by Bow Bridge. The plaque (*right*) – which still survives today remounted next to the Victorian bridge – reads 'Near this spot lie the remains of Richard III, the last of the Plantagenets, 1485.' In 1862, when the old medieval bridge was dismantled, navvies discovered a skeleton in the river sediments by the bridge. This led to a claim that 'King Dick' had been found, although within days of the discovery the *Leicester Chronicle* reported that close examination of the bones suggested that they were probably those of a man in his early twenties, and so not likely to be Richard III.

But where did Speed get the story from in the first place? He acquired material for his book from a wide number of sources: collections of original manuscripts, some now lost; from field observations; and from the works of other historians, including Sir Thomas More. None of them make reference to either legend, despite writing in some detail about Richard III's death and burial. Speed may have acquired tales from local oral tradition, but it is unclear whether he ever visited Leicester and it is possible that they were a creation of his own. Perhaps tellingly, Robert Herrick, who owned the friary site in the early 17th century and had erected a memorial to Richard in his garden, appears to have thought otherwise. Born in Leicester in 1540, whilst the friary was still being demolished, Herrick would have had the recollections of contemporaries to help him position his monument in the correct spot. If anyone in early 17th-century Leicester knew where Richard III was buried, it was surely Robert Herrick.

The 'King's Coffin'

One piece of Richard III's tomb widely believed to have survived destruction is the stone coffin in which his body supposedly lay. Again, Speed is the first person to document this event, writing that it was 'now made a drinking trough for horses at a common Inn.' By all accounts it was a well-known visitor attraction. In 1654 the diarist John Evelyn visited Leicester, which he described as 'famous for the tomb of the tyrant, Richard III, which is now converted to a cistern at which (I think) cattle drink', whilst another visitor in 1700, Celia Fiennes, wrote 'I saw a piece of his tombstone he lay in, which was cut out in exact form for his body to lie in; it remains to be seen at ye Greyhound in Leicester but is partly broken.' However, by the time the historian William Hutton visited Leicester in 1758 to see the trough 'which had been the repository of one of the most singular bodies that ever existed', he found that 'it had not withstood the ravages of time.' By then it was supposedly kept at the White Horse Inn on Gallowtree Gate.

Tellingly, the description suggests a style of coffin that pre-dates the fifteenth century, so it is unlikely to have had anything to do with Richard III. When monastic sites were redeveloped after the Dissolution it is probable that stone coffins would have been unearthed and it would seem that an enterprising innkeeper with an eye for business got hold of one as a potential tourist attraction for his establishment.

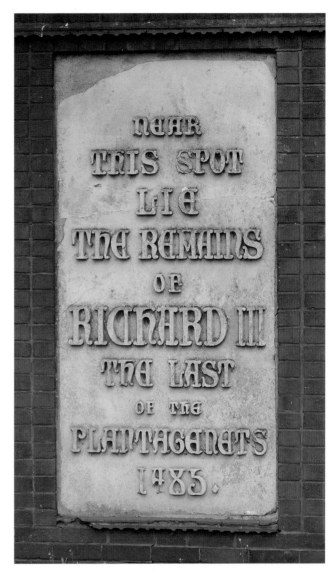

Above: 'The Victorian memorial plaque to Richard III, re-erected beside the present Bow Bridge.

Doing the groundwork

Urban archaeological excavation is a time-consuming and costly business. Towns like Leicester, which have a long history going back over 2000 years, can have very deep and complex archaeological deposits, in places reaching several metres in thickness. Constant cycles of demolition, redevelopment and recycling of building materials in the Roman and medieval periods, together with damage from foundations, cellars and sewers in more recent times means that the surviving archaeology is usually very fragmentary.

In Leicester, the evidence for walls normally only comes from 'robber trenches' – the ghost lines of where walls used to be, all stone from the superstructure and foundations having been removed long ago for re-use elsewhere, leaving the line of the original foundation trench backfilled with unwanted debris. Similarly, floor coverings worthy of salvage, such as tiles, are almost invariably found to have been stripped bare leaving behind only the mortar bedding. Hence, archaeological evidence for buildings is not only incomplete due to the recycling of materials, but has also very often suffered considerable damage from later disturbance. All of this of course makes it very complicated and it takes time to disentangle the sequence of deposits and excavate them by hand. This is why it is extremely important to do plenty of background research before considering putting a shovel in the ground, in order to maximise our chances not only of digging in the right place, but also in avoiding known disturbances.

The Greyfriars site was treated like any other potential urban investigation in the city. Philippa Langley was advised in the first instance to commission a 'desk-based assessment' to research all records of archaeological findspots in the vicinity, check the historical accounts and document the way the site has changed over the past few hundred years using historic maps. Like many cities, Leicester has a *Historic Environment Record* that contains information about previous archaeological excavations, observations and chance finds. This helps us to predict the depth of archaeological deposits surviving below the present ground level and in some instances narrow down the search for a particular site.

Mapping the way…

By comparing maps of the Greyfriars area drawn at different dates and different scales over the last 400 years, we can work out how the site has changed over time. The first maps of Leicester date to the early 17th century, but these show too little detail to be of much use. One map, produced by John Speed in 1610, even shows Grey Friars in the wrong place, mislabelling the Dominican friary of Blackfriars in the town's north-west quarter rather than the real site in the town's south-east quarter.

One map in particular proved invaluable: Thomas Roberts' 1741 map is the earliest surviving map of Leicester to show accurate detail of the Greyfriars area (*below*), clearly depicting a large enclosure labelled 'Gray Fryers', which is undoubtedly the friary precinct. Although the map dates to 200 years after the friary, it is believed that the land boundaries remained unchanged (a pretty

Left to right: an extract from Thomas Roberts' 1741 map of Leicester, showing the grounds of the 'Gray Fryers'; a modern map of the same area; the two maps overlaid, showing the 'Gray Fryers' (red) in relation to modern buildings and streets and three large open areas potentially available for excavation (dark blue).

commonplace occurrence) when Robert Herrick built his mansion and gardens here. These later buildings can be seen on the map.

Computer aided design (CAD) programs allow us to scale and orientate Roberts' map to match modern maps of Leicester. By identifying matching landmarks (i.e. roads such as Friar Lane and Cank Street, buildings such as St Martin's cathedral and the guildhall, property boundaries etc), the two can be overlaid and compared with a high degree of accuracy. Such Map Regression Analysis shows which parts are covered with modern buildings, and which parts today are still open areas that appear to have remained largely undisturbed since the friary was demolished in the 16th century.

Other sources

Old maps of Leicester: William Stukeley's 1722 map of Leicester (*extract right*) clearly marks 'Gray Fryers' in a block of land south of St Martin's church. Thomas Roberts' 1741 map of Leicester marks 'Gray Fryers' (*previous page*) in the same place.

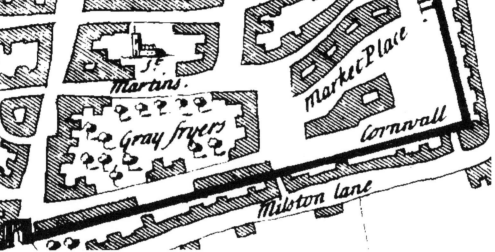

Medieval street names: Old street names provide clues to finding the friary. In the south-east 'historic' quarter of the city are two roughly parallel streets. These once ran between the Saturday market and the medieval High Street (today Highcross Street). The northernmost was called St Francis' Lane (today Peacock Lane), whilst the southernmost is called Friar Lane. These names suggest that a Franciscan friary once stood in the vicinity.

The murder of William of Loughborough in 1300: One medieval clue to the location of Grey Friars church is a Coroners' Roll, which lists all sudden deaths in Leicester. On 26 December 1300, William of Loughborough was viciously assaulted in the street by two men. One, only identified as Adam, shot William

in the back with an arrow, whilst the other, Richard Smith, struck William with a sword, severing the fingers on his left hand. William's body was found by his wife, Hawisia, who raised the alarm. Both men fled but were later caught and Smith was taken to Warwick prison. We do not know what finally happened to them. The street where the assault took place is described as 'the lane which leads to St Martin's church and towards the church of the Friars Minor.' This may refer to St Francis' Lane, thus suggesting Grey Friars church lay on the north side of the friary opposite St Martin's church.

John Leland's *History of Great Britaine*, c. 1543: Leland was a 16th-century antiquarian who travelled around England compiling material for a *History of Great Britaine*. In this he wrote 'the Grey Freres of Leicester stode at the end of the hospital of Mr. Wigston'. Leland may have visited Leicester whilst the friary was still occupied, or shortly after it was demolished. He places the friary south of Wyggeston's Hospital, built in 1513. This building, which was not demolished until 1875, is clearly shown to the west of St Martin's church on Roberts' 1741 map of Leicester (*previous page*) and the site on which it stood is still labelled on maps in the 1950s. This led the Ordnance Survey to mark *'Franciscan Friary (site of)'* in the New Street car park, just west of the Social Services car park where it was eventually found.

John Throsby's *History and Antiquities of Leicester*, c. 1791: Throsby was a noted local 18th-century antiquarian who wrote a book on the history of Leicester. In this he noted that 'the Franciscan or Grey Friary, stood on the south side of St Martin's church-yard… the grounds belonging to the Friary were spacious and extended from the upper end of the Market Place to the Friar Lane meeting house'. He also placed the church beneath houses facing St Martin's church (today 6–8 St Martins) because human bones were found there when workmen were digging their cellars.

Above: *Extract from William Stukeley's 1722 map of Leicester. Stukeley clearly labels 'Gray Fryers' in a block of land to the south of St Martin's church.*

Previously on this site…

Today much of the site is built on. Many of the historic buildings are protected and are unlikely to be demolished, such as the former Alderman Newton's Boys School (*right*). This was originally situated near St Nicholas' Church but by 1863 it had grown too big and a new place was needed. A site south of St Martin's was chosen, described by one of the trustees as 'central, very open and salubrious and in the neighbourhood of several large gardens'. The new building was designed in perpendicular Gothic style by the architects Goddard & Son; construction began in 1864, with the new school opening by the end of the year.

Alderman Newton's Boys' School closed in 1884, but the building remained in educational use, first as part of Wyggeston's School, then as Alderman Newton's Girls' School (1920–59) before ending up as Leicester Grammar School until it moved to a new campus in 2007. The site has now been purchased by Leicester City Council for a Richard III heritage centre.

Another notable building is No. 17 Friar Lane. Described as 'the handsomest Georgian house now left in the old town', No. 17 Friar Lane (*left*) was built during the latter half of the 18th century as a town house for a well-to-do merchant called William Bentley. Bentley never took up residence; he defaulted on payments and the house was repossessed and sold on. In the mid 19th century it was occupied by Dr Thomas Benfield and his wife Eleanor. At that time it contained an outer and inner hall, dining room and large drawing room; on the ground floor was the doctor's consulting room, surgery and dispensary, with wine and coal cellars beneath. The house had seven bedrooms or dressing-rooms, with box-rooms and smaller bedrooms for servants in the attic. The 1861 Census shows that the Benfields employed a live-in dispensing assistant, cook, housemaid, footman and errand-boy.

Above: The old Alderman Newton's School building today, heavily modified, with the 2012 excavation under way in the former playground.

Left: No. 17 Friar Lane today, looking north-west along Friar Lane.

*Opposite: A view of Leicester taken from St Martin's steeple in 1867, looking south. In the foreground is Alderman Newton's School (**1**) before it was extended in 1887 and 1897. To the left, behind the school is Robert Herrick's mansion (**2**). King Richard's grave was found in the garden to the right of the school (**3**). At the end of the garden is No. 17 Friar Lane (**4**). New Street can be seen on the right of the photograph (**5**). Image in Leicester Record Office.*

Where to dig?

Three areas were potentially available to us within the friary precinct: the Social Services car park, the former Alderman Newton's School playground and a private car park to the west of New Street. Apart from the costs of the investigation itself – hire of machinery to remove modern overburden, and employing archaeologists to excavate, record what was found and write up the results – the budget would also need to cover alternative car parking for displaced vehicles, plus reinstatement of the trenches at the end of the dig. The limited funds available would cover the costs of digging three trenches, each about 30m long by 1.6m wide, and we would need to locate them carefully to maximise the chances of finding any evidence of the friary.

The starting point was to look at other friary plans, to try and predict the positions of the principal buildings. However, whilst there are generally standard layouts for such sites – usually with the west–east orientated church to the north of the cloisters, as at Walsingham (*right*) – plans were often adapted to suit the space available. So the church, for example, could sometimes be on the south side, as it is at Leicester's Augustinian friary near West Bridge, or at the friaries in Bangor, Beverley, Bristol, Cardiff and Norwich. A plan of a notional church and cloister was laid over the modern Ordnance Survey map to get a feel of how much of the precinct was likely to be taken up by these buildings. On the basis of a typical arrangement with church either to the north or indeed to the south, Richard Buckley thought that two trenches aligned north–south on the eastern side of the

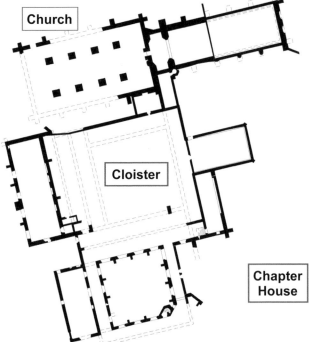

Church

Cloister

Chapter House

precinct, down the middle of the Social Services car park (*left*), would be the best strategy to pick up some of the many east–west walls. If this proved successful, a third reserve trench would then be dug to help clarify the building plans or even potentially target the choir in the (rather unlikely) event that the church was found. So this was to be the plan from the beginning, included in the Written Scheme of Investigation of 1 June 2011, with the proviso that it might be subject to alteration depending on the results of a Ground Penetrating Radar survey commissioned by Philippa and undertaken in August 2011.

All three available areas within the Grey Friars precinct were surveyed, revealing modern utilities such as electrical cables, water pipes and sewers, together with a number of more

Above: Plan of the Franciscan friary at Walsingham in Norfolk, a fairly standard friary layout. Scaled to match car park plan (left).

Left: Results of the Ground Penetrating Radar survey, showing the position of modern utilities (red) and ambiguous features (green); and the proposed locations of the first two trenches (black).

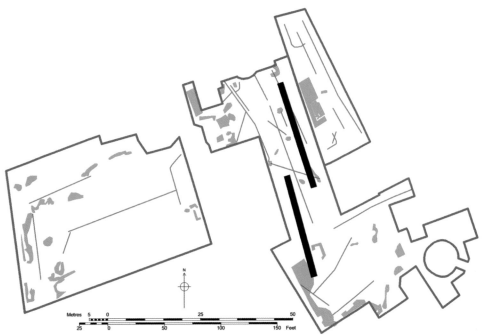

Metres 5 0 25 50

25 0 50 100 150 Feet

N

ambiguous features, but unfortunately no clear building plans emerged. It was thought that a layer of demolition rubble underneath the asphalt was probably masking any archaeological features. In view of this, there seemed no reason to change the proposed trench locations and the fieldwork was set to be done over Easter 2012, subject to funding and ongoing negotiations between Philippa and various television companies. Ultimately, it took longer than this to get the project off the ground and the work was put back to August and September 2012. By July, Philippa had not only secured most of the funding, but she had also persuaded Channel 4 to film the excavation, so the project looked as though it was on!

Richard Buckley now had to assemble his team to undertake the fieldwork and analyse the results. Mathew Morris – who had considerable experience of urban sites – was offered the job of supervising the fieldwork, assisted by another seasoned archaeologist, Leon Hunt, who had undertaken the background research on the Greyfriars site. Further members of the field team and volunteers would be sourced nearer the time, based on experience and availability. For the post-excavation work, our in-house team of Debbie Sawday (post-Roman pottery and tile), Nick Cooper (small finds), Jennifer Browning (animal bone) and Heidi Addison (finds processing and archiving) would look after the bulk of the material. Back in 2011, Dr Turi King, a geneticist specialising in genetic genealogy, had expressed an interest in undertaking this part of the work. Human osteologist Dr Jo Appleby was approached by Richard Buckley shortly before the excavation started and in his email of 17 August he said: 'Whilst I think it is rather unlikely that we will actually find the remains of the king – given that we are not sure

Chances of success?

The Greyfriars Project had five progressive research objectives:

1. Find the remains of the Franciscan friary.
2. Identify clues to the position and orientation of the buildings.
3. Within the friary, locate the church.
4. Within the church, locate the choir.
5. Within the choir, locate the mortal remains of Richard III.

To achieve all five goals was always going to be difficult. Because modern buildings and roads could not be dug up, the archaeologists could only excavate within an area covering approximately 17% of the identified friary precinct. With even further constraints of time and resources available to them, this meant that, in reality, they could only hope to excavate approximately 1% of the friary precinct.

Bearing this in mind, it was thought **Objective 1** was a reasonable expectation; **2** was a probability; **3** was a possibility; **4** was an outside chance; and **5** was not seriously considered possible.

where the church is, where he was buried and whether his remains were exhumed at the Dissolution – we need to be prepared! So the reason for writing is to ask whether you would be prepared to act as the project osteologist?' Jo replied, saying 'Well, that's definitely one of the more unusual emails in my inbox today' and although she would be away for the first week of the dig, would be very happy to be involved.

Work gets going

On Friday 24 August 2012, the Greyfriars Project was formally launched with a press conference and media opportunities, attended by Michael Ibsen, a direct descendant of Richard III's sister, who kindly agreed to provide DNA. Site director Mathew Morris and archaeologist Leon Hunt laid out the first two trenches and supervised the cutting of the car park surface with a road cutter.

Left: Lead archaeologist Richard Buckley explains the project to the media, watched by Michael Ibsen (a distant relative of Richard III) and Philippa Langley.

The 2012 excavation

Week 1 – Saturday 25 August

The project begins with the digging of Trench 1, which is 1.6m wide and runs for 30m approximately north–south in the Social Services car park. Before digging begins, a CAT scanner is used to identify any live electrical cables under the ground so they can be avoided. At first, ground beneath the car park appears to be very disturbed and brick and concrete wall footings for buildings dating back over the last 100 years have to be removed to reach the medieval archaeology beneath.

The first noteworthy discovery is a human left leg bone at the edge of the trench – a good find but not particularly surprising when excavating near a church. This is found approximately 5m from the north end of the trench, about 1.5m below modern ground level. Careful examination reveals a parallel right leg, indicating an undisturbed grave (pleasing, but again not unexpected). The remains (**A**) are covered to protect them from the weather until more is known about where they were located within the friary. In hindsight, the rather Shakespearean thunderstorm that heralds the discovery and the letter 'R' painted in a parking bay nearby prove to be rather portentous!

Trench 1 is incomplete at the end of the day due to a two-hour delay when the digger throws a track; however, results are promising. Archaeologists have uncovered a patch of disturbed ground (**B**), an east–west robbed wall (**C**) with possibly part of a low stone wall alongside it, and large quantities of medieval building rubble, all suggesting the presence of an important medieval building in the vicinity, most likely part of the friary.

✓ **Objective 1 achieved: the friary buildings located**

Sunday 26 August

Trench 1 is completed, revealing a second robbed wall (**D**), running parallel with **C**. Unfortunately, the presence of a live electrical cable running over the top of it makes it impossible to investigate further with the digger.

Above left: Archaeologists remove the car park and the remains of Victorian buildings with a digger to reach the medieval archaeology beneath.

Centre left: Fieldwork director Mathew Morris finds human bone in Trench 1.

Below left: Archaeologist Tom Hoyle removes medieval rubble in Trench 1.

Trench 2 is dug, also 30m long, parallel to Trench 1 and overlapping it by a short distance. At the southern end are the remains of a north-south orientated stone wall (**E**); at the northern end is a second, parallel north–south robbed wall (**F**), joined at right angles to a continuation of wall **D**. The space between **E** and **F** is relatively narrow (c. 2m wide), suggesting a corridor or two buildings built close to one another. More rubble masks the medieval archaeology, leaving it unclear which idea is correct until the building debris can be removed.

Monday 27 to Friday 31 August
Throughout the week, the archaeologists carefully remove dumps of building rubble left behind when the friary was demolished, exposing the medieval buildings beneath. These remains are planned, recorded and photographed, and features of particular interest are excavated to learn more about the friary.

In Trench 2, rubble is removed from between walls **E** and **F**, exposing the bedding for a tiled floor that steps down from south to north. Tile impressions can still be seen in the mortar, providing clues to how the floor would have once looked. Part of a stone step survives. At the southern end of the trench, wall **E** is found to survive partially intact above floor level, a rare discovery in Leicester. The remains of a doorway are found, leading through it from west to east.

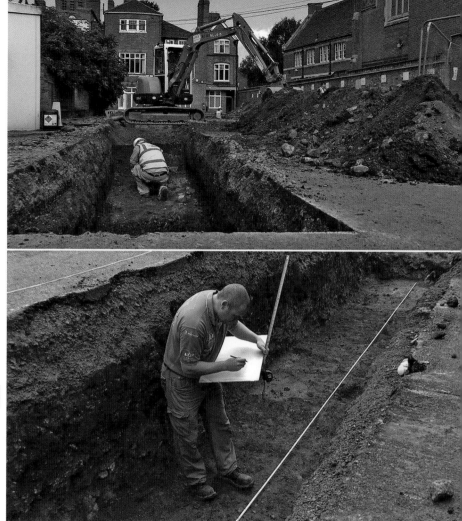

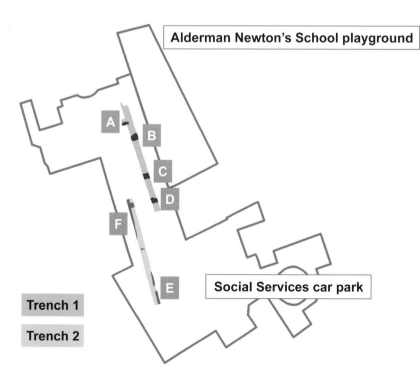

Alderman Newton's School playground

A
B
C
D
F
E

Social Services car park

Trench 1

Trench 2

Top: Whilst digging Trench 2, the top of a medieval stone wall is uncovered (E).

Above: Martyn Henson carefully plans and records the medieval deposits in Trench 2.

Right: A medieval silver penny found in modern garden soil over the friary. Sadly, it is badly worn and cannot be closely dated.

Above: Tile impressions can still be seen on the mortar floor bedding inside the cloister walk (E–F).

Above: Part of a stone step is found inside the cloister walk (E–F).

Above: Part of a stone wall and floor survived in Trench 2 (E). The remains of a doorway can be seen to the right of the photograph.

Left: A stone bench in the chapter house (C) with a curved 'bullnose' lip to the seat.

It appears that Trench 2 has, by chance, been dug along a long north–south corridor. Could the space between **E** and **F** represent one of the friary's cloister walks? If so, is it on the western or eastern side of the square courtyard or 'cloister garth'?

Back in Trench 1, archaeologists discover that the surviving low stone wall at **C** has a flat top with a curving 'bullnose' lip on one side and no foundation. It looks like a bench built up against the north (robbed) wall of the building. Keyhole investigation of robbed wall **D** – carefully avoiding the live cable! – finds a second 'bench'. Between the two is evidence for floor tiling.

The benches are a major breakthrough, providing an important clue to which part of the friary has been found: this is a place where people could sit facing each other and talk. In a medieval friary, that would be the chapter house, which normally projected from the eastern side of a cloister, making the corridor or building joining it in Trench 2 part of the eastern cloister walk or east range.

✓ Objective 2 achieved: parts of the friary identified

North of the chapter house, the space between **C** and **B** appears to lie outside the friary buildings. However, the patch of disturbed ground at **B** contains lots of loose building rubble and may be a large robbed wall, possibly the southern wall of the church. Damage caused by modern cellars makes it difficult to interpret the remains.

Friday 31 August

ULAS applies to the Ministry of Justice, under the 1857 Burials Act, for permission to exhume up to six sets of human remains. The plan is to investigate only burials which are potential candidates to be Richard III: i.e. males in their 30s, buried within the eastern half of the church, ideally with potentially fatal battle injuries.

Week 2 – Saturday 1 September

The discovery of the chapter house and eastern cloister walk in the first two trenches means that parts of the church may be present in the car park or the school playground, but where to look next? Richard Buckley makes the decision to look in the school playground because of the evidence (**A–B**) at the northern end of Trench 1.

Trench 3, also 30m long, will look for a continuation of wall **B** and confirmation of whether it might be the south wall of the church. Broadly parallel to, and overlapping with, Trench 1, this new trench will hopefully be shallower and less disturbed than the others. Two substantial east–west robbed walls (**G** and **H**) are found, about 7.4m apart, of a thickness and separation consistent with a church, along with large areas of flooring and hints of further graves. The trench also reveals an area of paving made from medieval tiles (**I**).

✓ Objective 3 achieved: the church located

Walls **B** and **G** line up, meaning that the human remains found on the first day (at **A**) lie inside the eastern half of the church, quite possibly in the choir – where Richard III was reputedly buried. For this reason, those remains will be among those exhumed when the licence is granted.

Sunday 2 September
The archaeologists uncover more of the tile pavement in Trench 3. It appears to have been made re-using medieval tiles from the friary and is perhaps a path in the garden of Robert Herrick's mansion, which occupied the site after the friary was demolished.

Monday 3 September
The Ministry of Justice grants a licence for the removal of human remains.

Tuesday 4 September
A small area above the human remains in Trench 1 (**A**) is carefully widened with a digger to give archaeologists better access to the burial. Jo Appleby and Turi King begin carefully to remove the grave soil by hand. Work is slow, to avoid damage to the skeleton and by mid-afternoon it is clear that the skeleton will not be exhumed before nightfall. Work is halted for the day.

Meanwhile, archaeologists begin to widen Trench 3 between walls **G** and **H**, hoping to uncover more of the church and determine whether the burial is indeed in the church's choir. While removing the rubble in Trench 3, a small group of human bones is discovered, buried in a small pit. This was not a complete skeleton, but seems to be the remains of a single person, probably a woman. A grave must have been disturbed by workmen when the church was demolished, and the displaced bones reinterred out of respect for the dead.

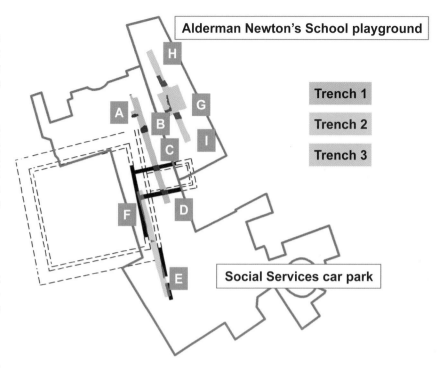

Alderman Newton's School playground

Trench 1

Trench 2

Trench 3

Social Services car park

Below: Kim Sidwell uncovers paving (I) that appears to be made from re-used medieval floor tiles and might be part of a path in Robert Herrick's garden.

choir stall base

tile impressions

graves

choir

north wall

south wall

step

presbytery

tile impressions

stone coffin

Finding King Richard III

Wednesday 5 September

In the school playground, archaeologist Leon Hunt and colleagues continue to expand Trench 3 between the two robbed walls (**G** and **H**). They find many broken decorated floor tiles and a sizeable pile of discarded pieces of tracery from a large stone window.

Over in the car park, Jo Appleby, assisted by site director Mathew Morris, begins carefully to uncover the skeleton in Trench 1 (**A**), first revealing the legs and the pelvis. There is no sign of any feet. Jo wears a special suit to prevent DNA contamination of the remains.

Back in the playground, two distinct spaces become evident in the church, represented by different patterns of floor tiling, still visible as impressions on the mortar bedding even though the tiles themselves no longer survive. There is a step up from the lower western floor to the higher eastern floor. Built into the lower floor is a narrow stone wall running parallel with the church's southern wall – perhaps the base of a choir stall. This would make the lower floor part of the choir (and hence the higher floor part of the presbytery).

✓ Objective 4 achieved: the choir located

While Leon Hunt and his colleagues uncover the church floor underneath the playground, back in the car park, Jo Appleby and Mathew Morris find that the grave in Trench 1 is not a neat rectangle but a rough, lozenge-shaped hole with untidy, sloping sides. It looks like it was dug quickly without great care.

Jo is surprised to suddenly uncover the skull at a much higher level in the grave than the rest of the skeleton. The head is bent forward and to the left at an awkward angle in order to fit the body into a grave that is slightly too short. There are obvious wounds on the cranium. Jo and Mathew realise that, whatever else is found, this skeleton is going to be both interesting and important.

In the afternoon, project manager Richard Buckley arrives with Deirdre O'Sullivan (an expert on urban friaries from the University's School of Archaeology and Ancient History) and an external specialist, Dr Glyn Coppack, who confirm the choir–presbytery theory and identify the pieces of stone tracery as in the style of an early 15th century 'perpendicular' window. Richard realises that the skeleton on the other side of the wall – the first find on the very first day of the dig – is actually buried within the choir.

Top: Archaeologist Jon Coward excavates a large pile of discarded stonework in Trench 3. It was initially thought that these pieces of carved stone came from an early 15th-century window in the eastern half of the church but it has now been proved that they actually date to the 19th century, and came from Alderman Newton's School.

Above: Osteologist Dr Jo Appleby carefully excavates the human remains in Trench 1 (A).

Left: Trench 3 (G–H) fully excavated, looking west. A medieval stone coffin and tile impressions in the presbytery can be seen in the foreground, with the remains of a choir stall behind.

Right: Jo Appleby examines Richard III's skull.

Below: Richard III's skull was propped up awkwardly against the end of the grave because it had been dug too short for him.

In the car park, Jo uncovers the arms and ribcage. The body has all the hallmarks of a hurried burial: there is no coffin, it has not been laid out carefully and the position of the bones suggests it probably wasn't even wrapped in a shroud.

Clearing away the earth from around the rib cage, Jo uncovers the base of the spine. Working along it, she finds a distinct bend to one side. As the rest of the spine is revealed, Jo and Mathew are somewhat shocked to see an unmistakable S-shape...

Mathew goes round to the playground to tell Richard that Jo has found something unexpected. Richard tells Mathew that he's busy with his guests but Mathew assures him, as calmly as he can and mindful of the crowd of bystanders peering through the playground gates, that he *really* does need to come and see what Jo has found.

Sometime later… long after everyone else has gone home, Jo and Mathew continue carefully to remove the skeleton, bagging and labelling each bone. As the last bones are lifted, one final discovery is made: a piece of rusted iron beneath two of the vertebrae. The skull, lower jaw and right femur, which will be used for DNA sampling, are wrapped in baking foil to protect them from contamination. Finally, with the sun setting, everything is loaded into the van, the gates are locked, and the mortal remains of Richard III bid farewell to the church of the Grey Friars after 527 undisturbed years.

Unbelievably…

✓ **Objective 5 achieved: Richard III found!**

Thursday 6 to Friday 7 September
Over the following days, the grave in Trench 1 is fully excavated and the archaeology around it is thoroughly investigated. Church floors matching those in Trench 3 can be seen in the sides of the trench and the north wall of the church is found at the very northern end of Trench 1. These suggest that the burial took place in the south-west corner of the choir, with the grave positioned against the southern choir stall.

In Trench 3, the remains of four or five other tombs are uncovered in the eastern half of the church. These date to a much earlier period of the friary's history. For this reason – and because a 'plausible candidate' has already been found – these graves are not investigated further, but are left undisturbed.

One of the graves contains a large trapezoidal stone coffin (*above right*), of a type dating from the late 12th century to the mid 14th century; considering its position in the church, not far from the high altar, it almost certainly contains someone of importance, perhaps a patron or benefactor of the friary. Although the coffin is not opened, a gap at its foot, between the lid and the base, allowed a glimpse inside. The feet of an articulated skeleton are partially visible inside the remains of what appears to be a metal coffin lining, probably of lead.

Week 3 – Saturday 8 September
The University of Leicester holds an open day at the site. Nearly 2,000 people attend, eager to learn about the excavation. Queues extend around the block (*right*).

Monday 10 to Friday 14 September
Further archaeological work, finishing the excavation and recording the archaeology.

✓ **Excavation complete**

Wednesday 12 September
A press conference at Leicester Guildhall announces to the world's media the discovery of the skeleton (*bottom right*). The press are then invited to visit the site and view the grave.

Saturday 15 to Sunday 23 September
Leicester City Council hold more open days. Thousands more people visit the grave site.

Monday 24 September
The vulnerable archaeology is covered with a permeable geo-textile membrane and hand-covered with soil to protect it, before the trenches are backfilled using a digger. A marquee is placed over the grave site to protect it from the weather. Greyfriars is once again a car park and a disused school playground.

The archaeologists now formulate their post-excavation programme, involving other specialists to undertake the scientific analyses that will prove that the Greyfriars skeleton is indeed Richard III.

44

King Richard's grave

Although the feet and one lower leg bone (left fibula) were missing – these had been removed long after burial, perhaps when a Victorian outhouse was built on top of the grave – Richard III's skeleton is otherwise complete, apart from a few small hand bones and teeth. It is amazing that there was so little damage, as in places, the 19th-century brickwork was just 90mm above the skeleton. If the Victorian workmen had dug much deeper or wider, Richard III's remains might have been severely damaged or even completely destroyed.

Richard III was buried at the west end of the church choir, in front of the southern choir stall (*right*). This location is slightly ambiguous. The choir is in one of the more important parts of the church, though not the most important (the presbytery), and it would have been very visible to the friars attending their daily services. However, this place was not generally accessible to the public, thereby preventing widespread veneration of the tomb. Out of sight, out of mind?

The irregular grave appears to have been hastily dug and was noticeably too short for the body, which had been propped up awkwardly at one end. Richard's body was not in a coffin and there was no evidence that he had been wrapped in a tight cloth shroud. Instead, he lay to one side of the grave, his torso and head crammed up against the edge (*opposite*). This would appear to tally with historical accounts suggesting that Richard III was buried rather unceremoniously (*see page 22*). However, it should also be remembered that he was killed in August and his corpse had been on display, unembalmed, for three days before burial. Decomposition would have already started and haste may have been a necessary practicality rather than lack of respect for the deceased.

The arrangement of the body suggests it was lowered feet first, head last. This explains why the legs are straight, but the upper torso and head are partially propped against the grave side. The way the hands are arranged, crossed at the wrist (most likely right over left) and placed askew above the right side of the pelvis is unusual. It is possible that they could have been tied together, either to keep the limbs tidy or perhaps because they were never untied after Richard III was taken down from the horse which transported his corpse back to Leicester.

No traces of clothing or personal ornaments were found in the grave. This is normal in medieval burials, although kings were often buried in their official robes with emblems of office. For instance, King John (d. 1216) was buried with a sword, whilst Edward I (d. 1307) was buried with a mortuary crown and sceptre. An iron object found under two vertebrae turned out, after closer examination and x-ray, to be a Roman nail. A few fragments of Roman pottery were also found in the grave fill, and it is likely that the grave diggers disturbed earlier archaeological levels, which became mixed up in the soil when the grave was filled in.

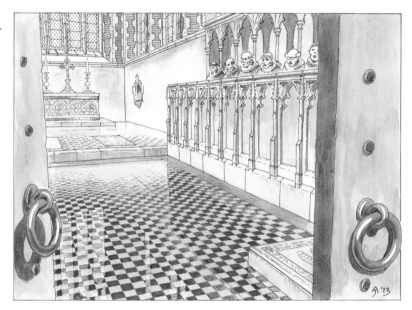

Above: Artist's reconstruction of the choir of the Grey Friars church looking east (top) and west (bottom), showing the arrangement of the choir and presbytery and the alabaster slab laid over the burial place of Richard III. Artwork by Jill Atherton.

Left: The king's remains in situ in his grave shortly after their discovery in 2012.

Above: Medieval masons take a moment for lunch, by Mike Codd. Reproduced by kind permission of Leicester City Council.

Putting the friary back together

Archaeology is like a fiendish jigsaw puzzle – one which consists of a mixture of several puzzles, each with half the pieces missing and with no picture to guide us! So first we have to try and disentangle the separate puzzles – in this case the individual buildings of the friary and different periods of building construction and refurbishment. Then within those, using the few pieces of the jigsaws that survive, try and reconstruct what the buildings looked like at different times.

With medieval religious houses such as friaries, we are at least fortunate in that there was generally a standard layout, albeit with some variation, meaning it is sometimes possible to predict building plans from quite limited remains. We can use archaeological evidence for the lines of walls – shown by surviving superstructure, foundations or 'robber trenches' (walls where all stone has been removed for re-use) – together with fragments of surviving floors to suggest the plans of individual buildings. Sometimes we can find evidence for the relative dating of structures, identifying alterations, extensions and episodes of demolition and rebuilding.

At Leicester's Grey Friars, the first trench revealed evidence for a pair of parallel east–west walls with stone benches built against their internal faces, identifying it as the chapter house – the only small building within the friary which would normally have fixed seating around the walls. The second trench revealed a pair of parallel north-south walls, a little over 2m apart, with flooring between, indicating a corridor which would have served the chapter house, thereby identifying it as the eastern cloister walk. At the southern end of this was a fragment of north–south wall surviving to a height of about 0.41m, perhaps part of the east range.

From this very limited evidence, it was then possible – by joining the dots – to propose a plan of the cloister garth, cloister walks and chapter house and suggest a position for the church either to the north or the south. The third trench tested this theory, and confirmed, with the discovery of substantial parallel east–west walls, that the church was indeed in its most common position on the north side of the cloister. Within the church, slender non-load-bearing east–west walls indicated supports for the timber choir stalls, whilst a step marked the junction between the choir and the presbytery to the east. Overall, the eastern half of the church (choir and presbytery) was 10.4m wide and at least 14m long, based on the predicted position of the 'walking place' immediately north of the east cloister walk.

Clues as to the appearance of buildings can come from such things as stone rubble, fragments of plaster, roof tiles, floor tiles, architectural fragments and window glass. Fragments of wall and areas of rubble showed that the friary was mostly built from grey sandstone, quarried locally from Danes Hill just 2km west of Leicester. Broken local Swithland slates, ceramic roof tiles and ridge tiles show that many of the roofs were tiled, whilst the documentary sources from the time of the Dissolution suggest that the church roof at least was clad in lead. Some excellent examples of apparently early Perpendicular window tracery of a style current in about 1400 were recovered from the Presbytery, but these came from a backfilled modern drain. Photographs of the 19th-century brick-built Alderman Newton School show that it originally had windows of just this type (*see page 32*), which had been replaced at some time in the 20th century, the originals being dumped on the (by then lost) site of the friary church, just to confuse 21st-century archaeologists!

Left: A plan of the Grey Friars friary, based on evidence from the 2012 excavation.

Plaster shows that some of the friary walls were rendered and whitewashed. Small pieces of broken window glass and lead came (metal strips that hold the glass in place) found amongst the rubble show that some of the windows were glazed. In most buildings, floors appear to have been covered with plain tiles laid in a diamond pattern (for a similar floor in Leicester Abbey, *see page 15*). These had coloured glazes in golden brown, orange and dark green. In the church, however, many of the tiles were highly decorated.

In the choir the tiles were laid in straight lines but in the presbytery they were laid in a diamond pattern. Many of the floor tiles were made near Nuneaton (27km to the south-west) whilst others were of a type more commonly found in south-west England, known as Wessex types. One Wessex design found frequently at Grey Friars appears to be that of an eagle displayed on a shield (*right*). This is the coat-of-arms of Richard of Cornwall (1209–72) or his son Edmund (1249–1300). Richard – the second son of King John – was Count of Poitou in France and the first Earl of Cornwall in England. He was a famous crusader, taking part in the Sixth Crusade (1240–3) and in 1257 he was also elected king of the Romans (king of Germany). His son, Edmund, the second Earl of Cornwall was an important figure at the courts of Henry III and Edward I. In 1272, Edmund leased the town and lordship of Leicester for four years from the Earl of Leicester. Whilst he, or conceivably his father, could have been benefactors of the friary, the tiles being deliberately chosen for this reason, it is equally possible that neither man had any specific connection. Heraldic floor tiles like this often represented popular chivalric designs of the period and were commonly sold as ready-made sets rather than being custom-made. Other motifs found on broken tiles among

the rubble of the church include heraldic creatures such as lions and griffins, fleurs-de-lys, and geometric and floral patterns.

Four pieces of monumental lettering and inlay cast in a copper alloy, possibly brass, were found around the church (*left*). Two represent individual letters – a 'D' and an 'E', one is a spacer or full stop, and one a broken strip perhaps from the border of an inscription. This style of lettering, with curved serifs, is known as Lombardic and dates to 1270–1350. The letters were probably once part of inscriptions adorning tombs inside the church. When the church was demolished everything of value, including this metal lettering, was salvaged so it could be melted down and recycled. During the process, a few letters were dropped and lost amongst the building rubble.

Other graves were marked by rubble-filled voids in the floor, showing where tombs or grave slabs had been removed when the church was demolished. In the choir these were located against the choir stalls and another was found against the north wall of the church in the presbytery. Beneath the voids graves could be seen. Significantly, none of these appears to have been disturbed, the destruction and defacement of the tombs being confined to floor level.

Finds of other objects which have been lost or discarded can provide indications of the function of individual rooms or buildings and sometimes provide details of the people who used them. At Greyfriars, however, such evidence was scarce, not only because the area excavated was small, but also because domestic finds such as pottery are not normally found on religious sites away from the domestic areas like the kitchen and refectory. From the church came two medieval silver coins which must have been dropped: one is too badly worn to date precisely (*see page 37*), but the other (*right*) is a halfpenny probably issued during the reign of King Edward IV, Richard III's older brother, and most likely minted in London in 1468–9.

At the time of the Dissolution in 1538, the cloistral buildings appear to have been in poorer condition than the church. Worn floors and evidence of significance subsidence to one of the walls south of the chapter house suggest that the friars did not have enough money to renovate their domestic accommodation. In contrast, the church shows evidence of numerous costly phases of reflooring, renovation and redecoration that took place through the building's 300-year

life. It is possible that the friars were only able to attract external patronage for work on the church.

Following the Dissolution, the friary was stripped of all valuable materials – such as lead from the roofs, windows and guttering – which would have been amongst the first material to be salvaged and melted down by the king's officers. Any movable furniture or wooden screens would have also gone rapidly, most sold off or recycled as firewood. Floor tiles, roof tiles and roof slates would have also been easy to remove and could probably be sold off more quickly than the stonework. Floor tiles in particular appear to have been widely reclaimed from the friary buildings, whilst the removal of roofing would have rendered the buildings uninhabitable.

This destruction was readily apparent in the excavations. Little trace of the actual friary buildings remained, even below floor level, with much of the stone from the walls and foundations removed for use elsewhere. Destruction of the church appears to have been particularly thorough, most likely conducted soon after the final surrender to prevent the friars resuming their daily liturgical routine. Soil accumulating inside the other friary buildings, however, suggests that they had been made roofless and uninhabitable, but left standing as ruins until a need for their stonework was found. There was no evidence of continued occupation of the buildings after the Dissolution, although this cannot be ruled out entirely, on the basis of the small area explored.

Left: A late 19th-century photograph reputedly showing part of an early 16th-century stone and brick wall on Peacock Lane, possibly the northern boundary wall of the friary. Sadly, this last surviving fragment of the friary was demolished in 1928 when Peacock Lane was widened.

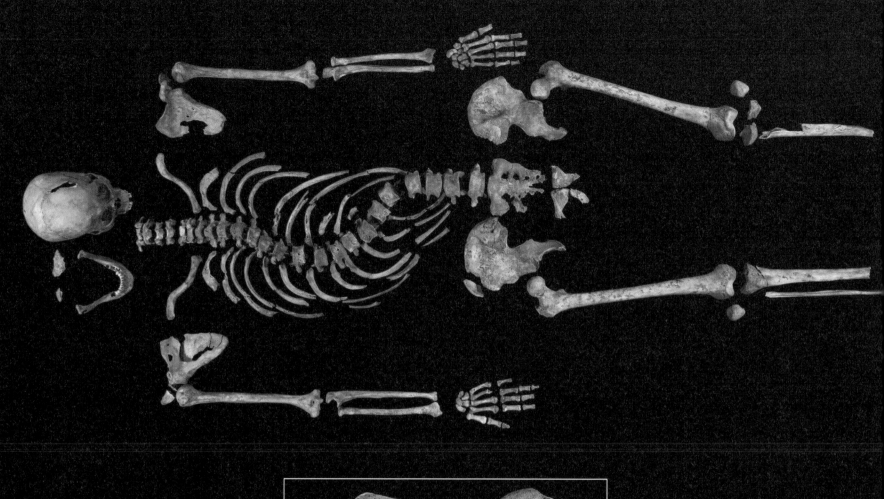

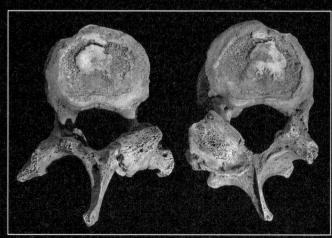

The skeleton of King Richard III

Back at the University of Leicester, specialists start to analyse the skeleton. As well as determining the age and sex of the individual, the spinal abnormalities have to be identified and the wounds characterised.

The bones are those of an adult male aged between his late twenties and late thirties. Richard III was 32 when he died. From the length of the intact right thigh bone (femur) it can be calculated that he would have stood about 5ft 8in (1.74m) tall, slightly above average for men during the medieval period (5ft 7in or 1.71m). However, the curved spine would have reduced his height significantly, making him appear much shorter. Overall, the skeleton is quite slender for a man, but there is no skeletal evidence for the limp or withered arm favoured by authors such as Sir Thomas More or William Shakespeare. Several teeth were lost before death; the rest are lightly worn, with some calculus (calcified plaque) and a few cavities.

A very pronounced curve in the spine was visible when the body was first uncovered, evidence of scoliosis, which may have meant that Richard's right shoulder was noticeably higher than his left. Further evidence of scoliosis can be seen in many of the individual vertebrae. These bones should be symmetrical, but many of the vertebrae have abnormalities in their shape (*left*).

The type of scoliosis seen here is known as idiopathic adolescent onset scoliosis. Idiopathic means that the reason for its development is not entirely clear, although there is probably a genetic component. The deformity was not present at birth, but developed during growth. The scoliosis may have been progressive, getting worse as Richard aged, but it clearly did not stop him from leading an active lifestyle.

Overall, the skeleton's physical attributes match the little we know about Richard III's age and appearance.

How Richard III was described by people who met him

'...he [Richard] was small of stature, with a short face and unequal shoulders, the right higher and the left lower.'

John Rous, late 1480s (chantry priest and chronicler)

'King Richard is... a high-born prince, three fingers taller than I, but a bit slimmer and not as thickset as I am, and much more lightly built; he has quite slender arms and thighs, and also a great heart.'

Niclas von Popplau, 1484 (itinerant Silesian knight visiting England)

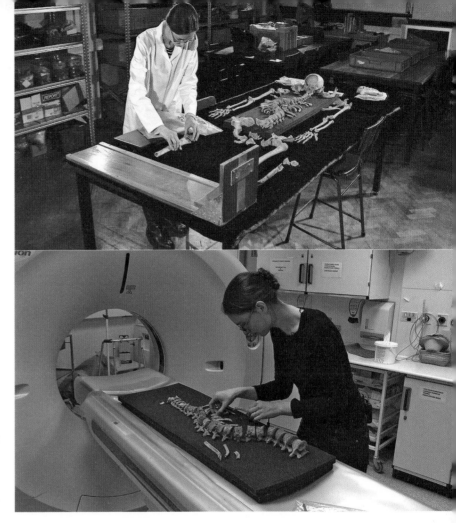

Top: Osteologist Jo Appleby lays out the remains of Richard III for analysis.

Above: As part of the forensic analysis, the skeleton was CT scanned (computed X-ray tomography) at the Leicester Royal Infirmary. Higher resolution Micro-CT scanning was also undertaken at the University's Department of Engineering. This has generated a lasting record of the skeleton, which can be studied long after Richard has been reburied. It will allow the bones to be examined in great detail, in particular the visible wounds and the effect of the scoliosis.

Left: The complete skeleton, showing the curve of the spine.
(inset) Two vertebrae showing abnormalities relating to the scoliosis. The spinous processes of the vertebrae (pointing down), which should be straight, are twisted to one side. The joints between the vertebrae show signs of osteoarthritis.

Injuries on the skeleton

After excavation, the bones were carefully cleaned with water and soft brushes. This revealed more significant injuries on the skeleton, to add to those visible when the remains were first uncovered. At least ten injuries have been identified. We cannot determine in which order the injuries were received – all that we can say for certain is that all of them happened at around the time of death (perimortem), as there is no indication that any had started to heal. It is not possible to distinguish between skeletal injuries occurring just before death and those occurring just afterwards. Interpretation of the wounds relies on knowledge of medieval weapons and armour as well as on the bones themselves.

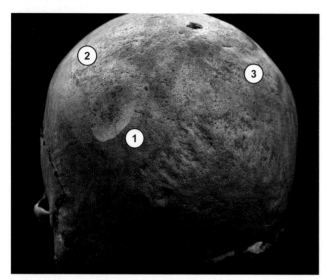

1–3. Wounds to left rear of skull and top of skull
A sharp bladed weapon or weapons has clipped the top rear of the skull several times, shaving off the top layer of bone, leaving small circular depressions. Close examination reveals striations from the blade.

4. Small penetrating wound on the top of the skull
A sharp blow from a pointed weapon such as a dagger on the crown of the head had enough force to split the inside of the skull, leaving two small flaps of bone.

5. Large hole underneath back of skull
The largest injury is this hole where part of the base of the skull has been completely sliced away. This could only have been caused by a large, very sharp blade wielded with some force. Whilst it is not possible to prove exactly which kind of weapon caused this injury, it is consistent with a halberd or something similar. An injury like this would have been fatal.

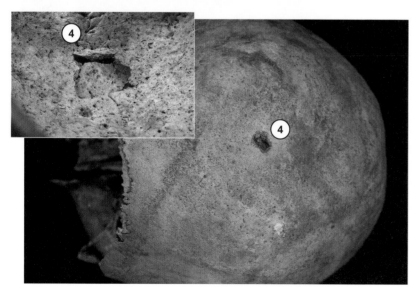

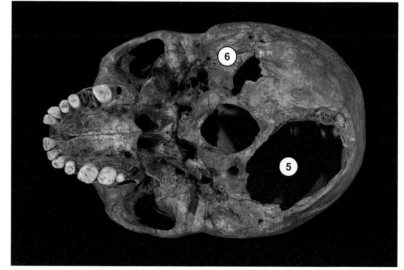

6. Wound on left base of skull

A second fatal injury, visible in the same photograph, is a jagged hole in the lower left side of the skull. A sword or similar bladed weapon has cut through the bone. Close examination of the interior of the skull revealed a mark opposite this wound, showing that the blade penetrated to a depth of 10.5cm.

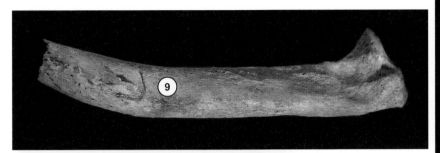

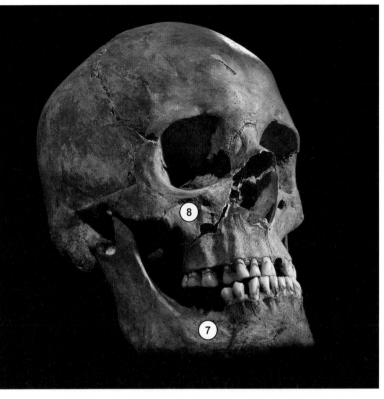

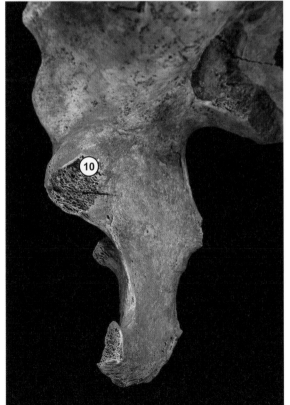

7. Cut on lower jaw

A blade has cut the right side of the chin.

8. Hole in right cheek

This rectangular hole may have been caused by a dagger or similar implement piercing right through the cheek.

9. Cut on one of the right ribs

This cut was caused by a sharp knife or dagger. During the battle the torso would have been protected by a solid armour backplate, so this may represent a post-mortem injury, perhaps delivered as a 'punishment' blow.

10. Cut on inside of pelvis

This was produced by a sharp weapon such as a sword or dagger. The weapon was thrust from behind, entering the right buttock and penetrating right through the body. Such a blow would be difficult to inflict during battle, when the king would have been protected by his armour. This injury may also have been inflicted post-mortem, as an act of humiliation.

Although it has been possible to identify numerous wounds on the skeleton, there are various other ways to injure or kill someone which would leave no mark on the bones and it is likely that Richard suffered additional wounds that have left no trace.

'Bloody will be thine end':* how Richard III died

From contemporary accounts of the Battle of Bosworth we know that Richard III led a mounted charge against Henry Tudor in an attempt to kill him and end the conflict. During this, Richard is credited as personally killing Henry's standard bearer, Sir William Brandon. This shows just how near he came to succeeding, as Brandon would have stayed close to Henry throughout the battle. However, momentum appears to have been lost when Richard III became mired in marshy ground, a feature confirmed by recent archaeological work on Bosworth battlefield (*see page 21*).

Whether because his horse became stuck or was killed we do not know, but Richard III appears to have dismounted and continued to fight on foot. But the tide of the battle was changing; the Stanley forces, ostensibly on Richard's side, now changed allegiance, leaving the Royalist forces outnumbered. Richard III fought on, despite pleas to flee, crying 'God forbid I yield one step. This day I die as a king or win!' but he must have become isolated from his bodyguard and surrounded by Henry's supporters who cut him down.

In the words of John Rous, 'if I might speak to the truth to his honour as a noble soldier, though he was slight in body and weak in strength, to his last breath he held himself nobly as his own champion, often crying that he was betrayed and crying, 'treason, treason, treason'...'

The early accounts generally agree that a blow, or blows to the head killed Richard, some crediting Welsh foot soldiers, armed with halberds or pole-axes, as the killers. Two are named, a Welsh noble called Rhys ap Thomas and a London skinner named William Gardynyr. The former was knighted after the battle, whilst Gardynyr was married to Helen Tudor, an illegitimate first cousin of Henry VII. Hence they may indeed be the men who killed Richard III, although we will never know for certain.

Some of these accounts are supported by the skeletal evidence, allowing us to explore possible scenarios for Richard III's dying moments. The physical remains tell us that Richard received multiple blows to the head from a number of different bladed weapons, particularly to the top, rear and base of the skull. These suggest he was ferociously attacked from all sides, probably by more than one person.

* Shakespeare's Richard III, Act IV, scene 4

None of the skull injuries (wounds 1–8) could have been inflicted on someone wearing a helmet of the type favoured in the late 15th century (*right*); so it would appear that Richard III lost his helmet, or that it was forcibly removed during the battle.

One massive, fatal blow (wound 5) could have been caused by a staff weapon such as a halberd, as contemporary accounts suggest; the trauma to the head matches accounts of his head being 'shaved' and that his 'brain came out with blood', as brain matter would certainly have been visible through this wound.

Wounds 5 and 6 both suggest that Richard was prone or on his knees with his head downwards when they were struck.

Interestingly, there are few wounds to the rest of Richard III's body. In particular, there are no defensive wounds on the forearms or hands. This may be further evidence that he was heavily armoured, the metal plate bearing the brunt of any blows. However, not all traumas leave marks on the bone and Richard may have sustained many more soft tissue injuries which left no trace.

Despite the head injuries, the king's face appears to have sustained little disfiguring trauma that affected the underlying bone. This may have been deliberate. It would have been important for the king's face to remain recognizable if he was to be publicly displayed, so people could witness and accept his death. An unidentifiable body would have defeated this purpose, and may have led to accusations that it was not the king's.

Some of the wounds would have been difficult or impossible to inflict if Richard III was still wearing armour and were therefore probably delivered after

he was dead. These include small wounds to the face (wounds 7–8), a stab in the back from behind (wound 9), and perhaps most tellingly, a stab wound to the buttocks (wound 10). Although it cannot be proved, these wounds may be symbolic 'insult injuries' delivered to the king's body after death; they would corroborate accounts that his body was treated less than reverently after the battle, when 'many other insults were heaped on it.' Polydore Vergil tells us that after the battle, Richard III's body 'naked of all clothing' was 'layd upon a horse back with the armes and legges hanging down on both sides.' It is easy to imagine then, the last and most insulting blow being delivered by a victorious Lancastrian soldier to the king's body as it was paraded back to Leicester.

Above: A modern re-enactor portraying Richard III at the Battle of Bosworth. He is dressed in metal-plate armour of a type common in the late 15th century.

Opposite: Richard III's last moments, illustrations by John Aggs.

Confirming the date of death

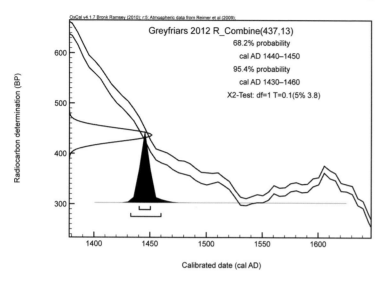

One of the first concerns after the skeleton had been discovered, was how old were the bones? Whilst the archaeological position of the burial made it clear that the grave was dug before the Dissolution of the friary in 1538, if the bones were centuries earlier than 1485 then they could not be Richard III's remains. Accordingly, one of the first pieces of scientific analysis to be carried out on the skeleton was radiocarbon dating.

This commonly used technique is based on measuring the minuscule amounts of radiocarbon (^{14}C) that are present in all living organisms, absorbed via carbon dioxide from the atmosphere that is taken up by plants, animals and humans. When an individual dies, uptake of ^{14}C stops. ^{14}C is an unstable isotope, which decays at a known and regular rate to a different form, ^{12}C. This enables the age of a sample to be calculated by measuring the proportion of ^{14}C now remaining. The development of accelerator mass spectrometry (AMS) means that even very tiny samples can now be dated directly.

Four small samples from one of the ribs of the Greyfriars skeleton were sent to specialist laboratories at the universities of Glasgow and Oxford for AMS dating. By testing pairs of samples at two different laboratories, the results could be internally and independently checked for consistency. Multiple dates can also be combined to achieve greater precision.

The initial results were very similar to one another: there was a 95% probability that the bone samples dated within the range cal AD 1430–1460 (Glasgow,

left) or cal AD 1416–1446 (Oxford). At face value, this person would appear to have died somewhere between a quarter and three-quarters of a century before Richard III. However, stable isotope analysis, carried out as part of the radiocarbon dating process, established that this person had a significant marine component in their diet (*see page 57*). Since marine-derived dates are on average 'too old' compared to equivalent 'terrestrial' dates, this had to be taken into account. The marine correction had the effect of making the date less precise, with a 95% probability that it falls within the range cal AD 1455–1640 (Glasgow) or cal AD 1447–1630 (Oxford).

The final stage of modelling radiocarbon determinations is to use Bayesian statistical analysis to combine all the relevant data, including in this case the archaeological end-date of burial before AD 1538. This narrows the date range down to cal AD 1455–1540 (95%), with a 68% probability that the date of death was between cal AD 1475–1530, which is compatible with the date of Richard III's death in 1485 (*below*).

Above left: Initial radiocarbon dating results from the University of Glasgow.

Below: The modelled radiocarbon results, taking into account all relevant data.

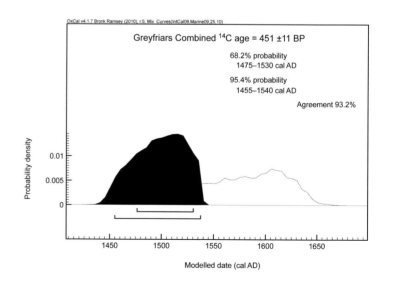

The royal diet and lifestyle

What Richard III ate

Many chemical elements exist in different forms, known as isotopes. By measuring the isotopes of carbon, nitrogen and strontium ($13C/12C$ and $15N/14N$, $87Sr/86Sr$) preserved in teeth and bone collagen, we can find out about the types of food and drink consumed during an individual's lifetime. Different parts of the skeleton can provide information about particular stages of a person's life. Samples were taken from Richard's teeth (which formed during his childhood and early adolescence), a femur (which averages his adulthood) and a rib (which represents the last few years of his life).

Oxygen and strontium values can be linked to the geology of the area where food was produced and to the water that was available to drink, and so determine a person's place of origin and any subsequent geographical movements. The oxygen data appears to confirm that Richard had moved out of eastern England, where he was born, by the age of seven, and then resided further west, possibly on the Welsh borders. Carbon and nitrogen tell us about the source of protein that was eaten – whether it came predominantly from plants or animals, and whether it was mainly terrestrial (land) or marine based (fish). Richard III evidently had a protein-rich diet, perhaps a quarter of which derived from seafood whilst much of the 'terrestrial' element was from meat.

By the mid 15th century, transport had become fast enough to allow wealthier inland householders to buy fresh sea fish, although preserved (salted or dried) white fish was far more commonly available. Finds of fishbones from Leicester excavations show that despite the distance from the sea, people ate marine species such as herring, cod, ling, haddock, dogfish and plaice at this time, as well as freshwater fish from the River Soar. In the medieval period, people were obliged to abstain from certain foods as a spiritual penance on the many Fast Days in the Christian calendar (every Friday and during Lent, for instance). For those who could afford it, fish made a good substitute for red meat and poultry. Analysis of skeletons from the medieval cemetery of St Peter's in Leicester shows that even people buried in high-status graves within the church ate less fish and considerably less meat than Richard III, the diet of most of the population comprising mostly cereals and vegetables.

So for most of his adult life Richard had a varied and protein-rich diet, typical of a late medieval nobleman who could afford to consume plenty of expensive foods like meat and fish. Differences in the values obtained from his femur and rib bone, however, suggest an increase in feasting and in the consumption of imported wine in the last few years of Richard's life. Kingship had evidently brought about a significant change in lifestyle.

Stomach troubles

As part of the investigation of his diet and health, soil samples were taken from within the gut area of Richard III's skeleton for microscopic analysis. This revealed the egg casings of roundworm, normally caught from human faecal matter as a result of poor personal hygiene or from contaminated food or water. The latter is most likely as there were well-established rituals of hand-washing amongst the nobility, whilst servants were perhaps rather less fastidious when preparing meals. We cannot be sure of the level of infestation – minor cases might have little effect on health, whilst severe cases can lead to severe bowel problems, malnutrition and stunted growth. Many people in medieval England would have carried this parasite.

Above: Preparing and serving a medieval meal. Scenes from the mid 14th-century Luttrell Psalter. © British Library, London.

Tracing a living relative

As soon as human remains were discovered in the Grey Friars church, it was evident that DNA analysis of the bones was going to be a crucial strand of evidence in confirming their identity as those of Richard III. However, analysis would be meaningless without something for comparison and therefore a living relative was required. When the search for Richard III was announced, the University of Leicester received numerous enquiries from people claiming to be related to the late monarch. Given the number of generations and the large families common in previous centuries, Richard's mother Cecily Neville could (mathematically) have several million direct descendants today. For a viable DNA comparison someone specific was required, either an all-male line descendant or a relative whose descent from Cecily Neville was by an entirely female line (*see page 60*).

There are no direct, all-male lines of descent from Richard III or his brothers. The last direct male descendant of the House of York was Richard III's nephew Edward, Earl of Warwick who was executed for treason in 1499. However, by tracing Richard III's family back four generations to Edward III (1312–77) an alternative all-male line of descent can be traced down through the Lancastrian side of the Plantagenet family, through John of Gaunt (1340–99) and his descendants, the Beauforts and the Somersets. Research of this line by Professor Kevin Schürer has identified a number of living male descendants of Henry Somerset, fifth Duke of Beaufort (1744–1803), whose Y-chromosome DNA should be consistent with Richard III's.

Male descent is often easier to trace in historical records, where the exploits of men are generally better documented than those of their wives and daughters. There is, however, one obvious pitfall. Although we can usually be certain who someone's mother was, the identity of their 'father' and their genetic male parent do not always coincide (either because of illegitimacy or adoption).

Fortunately, on the female side, a direct descendant of the House of York had already been traced. In 2003, as part of a project to identify the possible remains of Margaret of York (sister of Richard III and Edward IV), the historian John Ashdown-Hill traced an all-female line of descent from another sister, Anne of York, to a retired journalist in Canada, Mrs Joy Ibsen (née Brown). Mrs Ibsen passed away in 2008, but her son Michael, now living in London, very kindly provided a DNA sample as comparison for the Greyfriars project. However, in order to use Mr Ibsen's DNA as a benchmark, the all-female line of descent from Cecily Neville to Mr Ibsen needed to be independently verified. This task fell to Kevin Schürer.

Much of the early part of the family tree (*opposite*) is based on 'visitations', contemporary accounts by representatives of the College of Arms on families claiming the right to heraldic insignia awarded to previous generations. Many of these 'pedigrees' were collected and published by historians in the late 19th and early 20th centuries. Building on this earlier work, documentary evidence (in the National Archives and elsewhere) has been found for every link in the chain connecting Cecily Neville, Duchess of York (1415–95) to Michael Ibsen, furniture maker (born 1957). Wills, baptism registers, certificates of birth and marriage and even the passenger list for the *SS Mauretania*, which carried Joy Brown and her mother to Canada in 1948, together provide indisputable documentary evidence of an unbroken female line of descent.

During the genealogical research, Kevin Schürer also searched for and identified a second all-female line of descent from Cecily Neville to another living person, again with solid documentary evidence for every step of the way. Identification of a second line of descent would allow better corroboration of the genealogical and genetic results. This person agreed to participate in the project but wished to remain anonymous and is therefore referred to as 'Lineage 2'.

Below: Michael Ibsen, Richard III's great-nephew, seventeen times removed.

The family tree

Cecily Neville (1415–1495) Duchess of York
Great grand-daughter of Edward III and the common ancestor of all English monarchs from Henry VIII to the present day. Betrothed at the age of nine to Richard Plantagenet, her father's 13-year-old ward, they were married in 1429 when she was just 14. She bore him 13 children of whom seven survived to adulthood: Anne of York, Edward IV, Edmund, Elizabeth, Margaret, George and Richard III.

Anne of York (1439–1476)
At eight years old, she was married to Henry Holland, Duke of Exeter, who sided with the Lancastrians in the Wars of the Roses. They had one daughter but separated in 1464 and divorced in 1472. Two years later she married Thomas St Leger, a loyal follower of Edward IV who rose up against Richard III as part of the Duke of Buckingham's attempted rebellion. Anne died in 1476 giving birth to the couple's only daughter...

Anne St Leger (1476–1526)
In 1483 an Act of Parliament confirmed Anne as heiress to the estates of her father. About 1495, she married George Manners, Baron de Ros, who fought on behalf of Henry VII in Scotland and for Henry VIII in France. She bore him eleven children including...

Catherine Manners (c. 1500–c. 1547)
She married Robert Constable in about 1520. He was a soldier who fought against the Scots for Henry VIII in the 1540s and subsequently became MP for Yorkshire and then Sheriff of Yorkshire. The couple had eleven children including...

Barbara Constable (c. 1525–c. 1561)
First wife of Sir William Babthorpe. Suspected of Catholicism, Babthorpe proved his loyalty to Elizabeth I by helping to quell the 'Northern Rebellion' of 1569 which attempted to place Mary Queen of Scots on the throne. Among the couple's children was . . .

Margaret Babthorpe (1550–1628)
A devout Roman Catholic, she married Sir Henry Cholmley in about 1575 and the couple converted to Protestantism in 1603. Their daughter was…

Barbara Cholmley (c. 1575–1619)
She married Thomas Belasyse, Viscount Fauconberg, an ardent Royalist during the Civil War. They had seven children including…

Barbara Belasyse (1610–1641)
Her husband was Henry Slingsby, Baronet Scriven, a Royalist politician and soldier who fought at the Battle of Naseby and was beheaded in 1658 for his part in an attempt to restore the monarchy. The marriage in 1631 produced four children including…

Barbara Slingsby (c. 1633–?)
The second wife of Sir John Talbot, married in 1660, and mother of five children including…

Barbara Talbot (c. 1665–1763)
Married Henry Yelverton, viscount Longueville, in 1689 and lived to the ripe old age of 98. She had seven children including…

Barbara Yelverton (c. 1692–1724)
In 1715 she married Reynolds Calthorpe, High Sheriff of Suffolk and a Whig MP in the Parliaments of William III and Queen Anne. They had one son and one daughter…

Barbara Calthorpe (c. 1716–1782)
Married Sir Henry Gough in 1741. They had six children including…

Barbara Gough (c. 1745–1826)
Also known as Barbara Gough-Calthorpe, a name adopted by her brother Henry in 1788. She married Isaac Spooner, a wealthy Birmingham businessman, in 1770 and they had ten children including Barbara, who married anti-slavery campaigner William Wilberforce, and…

Anne Spooner (1780–1873)
Married Rev. Edward Vansittart-Neale, Rector of Taplow in Buckinghamshire, in 1809. They had eight children including Edward, one of the founders of the Co-Operative Society, and…

Charlotte Vansittart Neale (1817–1881)
In 1841 she married Charles Frere, a barrister and parliamentary clerk, and bore him nine children including…

Charlotte Vansittart Frere (1846–1916)
Married artist and writer A G Folliott-Stokes of St Ives, author of several important books on Cornwall, in 1882.

Muriel Stokes (1884–1961)
In 1919 she married Orlando Moray Brown. They had three children including...

Joy M Ibsen (1926–2008)
In 1948, Joy and her mother sailed to Canada where Joy worked as a journalist and later married newspaper editor Norm Ibsen. The couple had three children including...

Michael Ibsen (1957–)
A Canadian furniture maker who today lives in London

The DNA analysis

How could we use DNA in this case?

We all carry DNA in nearly every cell in our body and it can be used to identify us. For this case, however, there were a number of issues to consider. After death, DNA begins to break down and as time passes it becomes increasingly difficult, if not impossible, to retrieve for analysis. The survival of usable DNA often depends less on the age of the remains than on the environmental conditions in which they lie (e.g. moisture, soil acidity, temperature). Ideally, we want cold and dry conditions, something not commonly found in Leicester. Another consideration is the possibility of modern DNA contamination: any DNA left in the remains would be of low quantity and in tiny fragments. Handling the remains with bare hands would deposit large amounts of modern, intact DNA, which could easily overwhelm any signal from the skeleton's DNA. Therefore it was essential first to excavate the remains under clean conditions and then see if it was possible to retrieve any DNA from them. However, simply analysing DNA from the skeletal remains would not tell us who this individual was. We needed a relative of Richard III to compare the DNA to – and because of how our DNA is inherited, not just any relative would do.

Different parts of our DNA are inherited in different ways

Most of the DNA that we inherit is a mixture of that of our parents, which is a mixture of that of their parents, and so on back through time. As a result the vast majority of it is a complex patchwork of that of our ancestors, and after many generations, such as those which have passed since Richard III was alive, it becomes impossible to know which bit, if any, has been inherited from which ancestor. However, two pieces of our DNA have simple patterns of inheritance and do not mix over the generations and so could be used to compare the DNA from the Greyfriars skeleton with the DNA of particular living relatives today (we are all related to Richard III, it's simply a matter of degree).

The Y-chromosome contains the gene for maleness and therefore it can only be passed down from father to son through the generations, making it very useful in tracing male lines of descent. Conversely, mitochondrial DNA (mtDNA) is a small circular piece of DNA that is transmitted by a mother, in the ovum, to all of her children. Men inherit their mtDNA from their mothers but cannot pass it on; daughters, on the other hand, will pass it on in turn to all their children and so on down, and it is therefore very useful in tracing female lines of descent.

Why did we use mitochondrial DNA?

For this project, the primary interest was the mitochondrial DNA. This was for two reasons. First, there are many copies of our mtDNA in each cell (whereas there is only one copy of the Y chromosome), so there is a greater chance of the mtDNA surviving in sufficient quantities to successfully sequence – even after 527 years. Secondly, we already had a female-line relative of Richard III known to us, in the form of Michael Ibsen.

'I have to admit, I went really quiet when the first sequences started to come back and I could see that time and again it was matching. It was great; I got up and did a little dance around the lab!'

**Turi King, project geneticist
(reaction during public lecture)**

The modern-day relatives

Our mtDNA is transmitted from mother to child; as long as the female line remains unbroken, the mtDNA remains constant, barring small naturally occurring mutations. This means that Richard III and any of his siblings should all carry the same mtDNA type – inherited from their mother, Cecily Neville. If any of Cecily's daughters had daughters and as long as those daughters continued to produce daughters of their own (highly likely in an age when eight to ten children was common) down through the generations, the mtDNA will have been passed intact down those lines of descent. Michael Ibsen is a direct female-line only descendant of Richard III's eldest sister, Anne of York (though he himself would not be able to pass the mtDNA on to any children). Consequently, if the remains found in Grey Friars church were indeed Cecily Neville's son Richard III, the mtDNA present should match that of her great-great-great-great-great-great-great-great-great-great-great-great-great-great-great-great-great-grandson Michael Ibsen and that of Lineage 2 – because there are no males in either of their lines of descent from Cecily.

Testing modern DNA

Turi King carried out sequencing on the mitochondrial DNA from both Michael Ibsen and the second individual. If the genealogy was correct then a DNA match would be expected between them and this proved to be the case. The next step was to see if their mtDNA matched that of the skeletal remains.

Top left : Mr Ibsen provides a DNA sample for Dr Turi King.

Middle left: Turi King extracts Mr Ibsen's DNA in a laboratory at the University of Leicester. Whilst DNA from living people can be studied in a modern DNA laboratory, the study of ancient DNA requires special facilities, not least a completely clean environment, since the slightest trace of modern DNA can irretrievably contaminate a specimen.

Bottom left: Turi King and Gloria Gonzalez Fortes work in an ultra-clean ancient DNA laboratory at the University of York to extract the DNA from the Greyfriars skeleton.

Right: A chromatogram showing a small part of the matching mitochondrial DNA sequences of Michael Ibsen, Lineage 2 and the Greyfriars skeleton identified as Richard III. The full sequence is too long to show in its entirety.

Testing ancient DNA

After careful excavation under clean conditions from the Greyfriars site, the skull, the lower jaw and one femur (thigh bone) from the skeleton were placed for safekeeping in the clean room at the University's Space Research Centre – normally used for the construction of spacecraft components. This was to reduce the risk of any contamination of the remains with modern DNA. Due to their preservation, the teeth offered the best hope of intact mtDNA, with the femur kept as a secondary source.

Next, Turi travelled to two world-leading laboratories specialising in the study of ancient DNA – the University of York to work with Michael Hofreiter and the Université Paul Sabatier at Toulouse in France to work with Patricia Balaresque – with the work in both labs verifying one another. In these labs, DNA was extracted from teeth carefully removed from the skeleton's lower jaw. At all times, Turi and her colleagues had to remain suited up with gloves and masks to avoid any contamination with modern DNA.

The results

The first important result of the Y-chromosome DNA analysis was to prove that the skeleton does indeed have a Y-chromosome, confirming that the individual is male. This is important because it corroborates the results of the skeletal analysis.

Secondly, analysis of sequences in the control region of the mtDNA from the Greyfriars skeleton, Mr Ibsen and Lineage 2 revealed a match between them, as would be expected from the genealogy. All three share a type of mtDNA which is relatively rare in the population of Europe, adding further weight to the match. Therefore the DNA analysis is consistent with these being the remains of Richard III and provides another strand of evidence in the case.

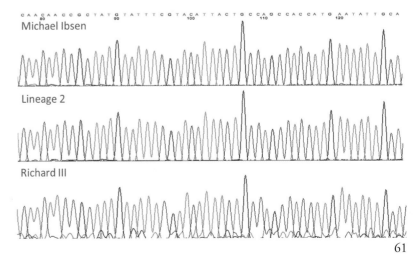

Conclusion

The discovery of the remains of Richard III at Greyfriars, Leicester in September 2012 generated an unprecedented amount of public and press attention for an archaeological project. Usually it is only finds of treasure or spectacular artefacts that attract such excitement and not, as in this instance, just a hastily dug grave containing the mortal remains of a 15th-century man. So what is it about Richard III that makes him stand out as an historical figure who is worthy of such widespread interest? The simple answer is that he is not only the most controversial monarch in British history, leading to vastly differing opinions as to his character, but also that there has long been a mystery surrounding the whereabouts of his grave.

History, they say, is written by the victors and Tudor writers and artists had no qualms about depicting Richard III as an evil tyrant and child-murderer, as well as a crippled hunchback; Shakespeare's eponymous play, written 106 years after his death, cemented the king's bad reputation (and appearance) right to the present day. More recently, however, this image of him has been questioned by many, and in 1924, the Richard III Society was founded by Saxton Barton, who wished to promote a more balanced view of the king, 'founded on facts where possible and on honest conviction'.

Whilst archaeology cannot contribute in any material way to the ongoing debate over the character of Richard III, what it has been able to do is solve the mystery surrounding his grave and provide new insights into his diet, health, appearance and the manner of his death. Excavation has shown that Richard received an apparently hasty burial at the west end of the choir of the church of the Grey Friars, with no coffin or shroud. His hands were very possibly still tied, as if his naked body had been taken down from the horse across which it was slung on the way back to Leicester and placed in the grave by the friars after a period of public display. Scientific analysis of the skeleton has shown it to be a man in his late twenties or thirties, of about 5ft 8in tall, with a slender build and severe curvature of the spine (scoliosis), which may have taken several inches off his height. He had a high-protein diet with significant marine content, identifying him as a member of the nobility, and died between 1455 and 1540 as a result of severe wounds to the head inflicted in battle. Further wounds to the skeleton may have been inflicted as insults after he

had died. These lines of evidence, taken together with a DNA match between modern descendants of Anne of York (Richard's elder sister) and ancient DNA extracted from the skeleton, enabled the University to announce on February 4th 2013 that the remains were indeed those of Richard III, the last Plantagenet king of England.

Archaeological projects invariably throw up more questions than were originally posed and this one is no different. There is still much to learn about the dating, development, architecture and destruction of Leicester's Franciscan friary, whilst the project has stimulated new debate about the character of Richard III and the nature of his death and burial which will clearly go on for many years to come. In July 2013, further archaeological investigation was carried out at the site of the Grey Friars church in advance of works to convert the former Alderman Newton's School into Leicester City Council's new King Richard III Visitor Centre. This opened in July 2014 and tells the story of the search for the King under the Car Park. Once the scientific analysis of the skeleton has been completed, the remains will be transferred into the care of the Cathedral of St Martin in Leicester (in accordance with the licence to exhume issued by the Ministry of Justice), a very short distance from the site of Grey Friars, where they will be reinterred with due ceremony on 26 March 2015.

Right: Facial reconstruction of Richard III, modelled by Professor Caroline Wilkinson of the University of Dundee. The bust is a representation of Richard's appearance based on scientific interpretation of the anatomical features of the king's skull. The work was commissioned by the Richard III Society.

Further reading

ASHDOWN-HILL, J. 2013 *The Last Days of Richard III and the Fate of His DNA*. Stroud: The History Press.

BALDWIN, D. 1986 King Richard's Grave in Leicester, *Transactions of the Leicestershire Archaeological & Historical Society* 60, 21–24.

BALDWIN, D. 2013 *Richard III*. Stroud: Amberley Publishing.

BENNETT, M.J. 1993 *The Battle of Bosworth*. Stroud: Sutton Publishing.

BILLSON, C.J. 1920 *Medieval Leicester*. Leicester: Edgar Backus.

BUCKLEY, R., MORRIS, M., APPLEBY, J., KING, T., O'SULLIVAN, D. & FOXHALL, L. 2013 'The king in the car park': new light on the death and burial of Richard III in the Grey Friars church, Leicester, in 1485, *Antiquity* 87, 519–538. http://antiquity.ac.uk/ant/087/ant0870001.htm

FOARD, G. & CURRY, A. 2013 *Bosworth 1485: A Battlefield Rediscovered*. Oxford: Oxbow Books.

LANGLEY, P. & JONES, M. 2013 *The King's Grave: The Search for Richard III*. London: John Murray.

MORRIS, M., BUCKLEY, R. & CODD, M. 2011 *Visions of Ancient Leicester*. Leicester: ULAS.

O'SULLIVAN, D. 2013 *In the Company of Preachers: The Archaeology of Medieval Friaries in England and Wales*. Leicester: Leicester Archaeology Monograph 23.

Acknowledgements

A project such as this could not have succeeded without the contribution of many individuals and organisations. University of Leicester Archaeological Services (ULAS) would like to take this opportunity to thank everyone involved, especially Philippa Langley whose inspiration and enthusiasm brought this project to fruition, together with Richard Taylor of the University of Leicester and members of the Richard III Society, including Dr Phil Stone, Dr John Ashdown-Hill and Annette Carson. From Leicester City Council, we should also like to thank the City Mayor, Sir Peter Soulsby; Sarah Levitt, Laura Hadland, Nisha Popat and David Orton from the Museum Service; Chris Wardle, City Archaeologist; Mick Bowers and all the Staff at Social Services for their help and understanding during disruption to the car park, and Nick Weston and Satish Shah of City Highways for the reinstatement of the trenches. We are especially grateful to David Brown of JoinPoint for organising the tarmac cutting, plant, fencing and crowd barriers, and to Steve Stell and Paul Finnegan for their masterly control of the mechanical excavator.

At the University, we received much support from press office staff Ather Mirza, Peter Thorley, Mark Riley Cardwell, Hannah Tucker and Debbie Evanson; the web team, Mike Simpson, Vic Russell and Michelle Heap; Graphics, Angela Chorley (who designed the cover); Alumni Development, Fran Wilson and Multimedia Services, Jon Shears and Carl Vivian.

Last but not least, we should like to thank all the many archaeologists, specialists and volunteers who contributed to the excavations and the post-excavation analysis: ULAS staff Heidi Addison, Steve Baker, Jennifer Browning, Nick Cooper, Jon Coward, Tony Gnanaratnam, Tom Hoyle, Leon Hunt, Anita Radini and Debbie Sawday; School of Archaeology and Ancient History staff Dr Jo Appleby, Professor Lin Foxhall, Dr Jackie Hall, Dr Turi King, Deirdre O'Sullivan and Dr Ian Whitbread; Professor Sarah Hainsworth and Richard Earp, Department of Engineering; Professor Guy Rutty, Forensic Pathology Unit; Professor Bruno Morgan, University Imaging Unit; Professor Kevin Schürer, Pro-Vice Chancellor for Research and Enterprise; Professor Jane Evans, Dr Angela Lamb, British Geological Survey; Dr Derek Hamilton, SUERC; Dr Piers Mitchell, University of Cambridge; Professor Christopher Ramsey, ORAU; Robert Woosnam-Savage, Royal Armouries; Professor Michael Hofreiter, Dr Gloria Gonzalez Fortes, University of York; Dr Patricia Balaresque and Dr Laure Tonasso, Université Paul Sabatier; and volunteers Pauline Carroll, Martyn Henson, Pauline Houghton, Karen Labniuk, Andy Mcleish, Kim Sidwell and Ken Wallace. Finally, a special thanks to Dr Patrick Clay, Vicki Score and Jackie Swallow for not only keeping ULAS running but also for their considerable help and support.

The book was designed and written by Mathew Morris and Richard Buckley with contributions from Jo Appleby, Turi King, Kevin Schürer and Mike Simpson and edited by Pam Lowther. She and Professor Colin Haselgrove made helpful suggestions on an early draft of the text, but the authors take full responsibility for any errors or omissions. Most of the site photographs were taken by Carl Vivian, with additional images taken by various ULAS staff and Colin Brooks; the aerial photograph on page 7 is by Webb Aviation. The painting of the interior of the Great Hall of the castle on page 12 is reproduced with kind permission of Joe Goddard, the portrait of Robert Herrick on page 26 is reproduced with kind permission of Leicester Arts and Museums Service, the photograph on page 32 was supplied by the Record Office for Leicestershire, Leicester and Rutland, and the artwork on page 54 by John Aggs is reproduced by kind permission of Leicestershire County Council.